## Acknowledgements.

Quilters are the nicest people, the world over. Special th[...] for kindness in the past year are due to Bonnie, Marge and Mike at Quilters' Resource in Chicago. Justine and Rostyn Jones, Dorothy and Terry Leadbeater, Christine and Brendan Moriarty and Diane Dolan in New Zealand ................... This one's for you.


**In addition further thanks are due to the following ...**

Sue Martin, Martin Mc Donald, Jane Plowman, and Alan Smith  for technical assistance.

Nora Field, Chris Graves, Jenny Hipperson, Alison King,  Sue Martin, Denise Matthews, Kathleen McMahon, Jane Plowman,  Carmen Redler, Shirley  Winchester, and  Judy Wilson, who,  after  agreeing to be 'guinea-pigs' for a workshop, kindly lent their resulting work to be photographed.

Empress Mills for providing some highly recommended machine embroidery thread in lovely colours for me to try in my featured examples .....
full range available by mail order... information from....
Empress Mills (1927) Ltd.  Hollin Hall Mill.  Trawden.  Colne.  Lancs BB8 8SS.

**'Pieceful Scenes'  c  1997  Angela Madden.**
**ISBN  0  952 1060  4  3.**
**First edition 1997.**

M.C.Q. Publications.
19, Barlings Rd.
Harpenden. Herts
AL5 2AL.
England.

### International Distributors.

| **U.S.A.** | **New Zealand.** | **Australia.** |
|---|---|---|
| Quilters' Resource Inc. | Margaret Barrett Distributors. | Books 'n Things. |
| P.O. Box 148850. | 19, Beasley Ave. P.O.Box 12-034. | Victoria. |
| 312 - 278 - 5795. | Penrose. | Tel. 03 94170052. |
| Chicago. Illinois 60614. | Auckland. | |

# Index.

# Introduction.

One of the most exciting aspects of being a Quilter is the variety of new techniques and ideas constantly being devised to keep us interested. The frontiers of patchwork are still moving forward. We have come a very long way from the humble beginnings of our craft, using up old and scarce scraps to make new utility items. Today, wonderful fabrics attract us in shops, and designing our next project can be full of fun, excitement and challenge. We can learn from, but should not be restricted by, tradition. We are lucky to have design and sewing aids that would have amazed our grandmothers. Tomorrow's traditions are being developed today. Experiment ....... try something new ..... and embrace the delights of colour and design with enthusiasm. Exciting techniques can be easy.

This book combines two aspects of quilt design which have always interested me: the creation of fabric landscapes and the manipulation of patchwork blocks to produce perspective illusions ..... 'Trompe l'oeil' ... a 'trick of the eye'. It seems to me that these concepts can be beautifully merged, giving rise to a new and exciting generation of quilts ......... 'magic windows.'

The overall principles are constant in these designs, but the content and colour choice can be original to the designer. Individual requirements for size and intricacy of pattern can be varied. If you incline towards a traditional appearance and gentle colours, make these the starting point for this technique ............ or opt instead for zany colours for 'eye popping' impact ......... the choice is yours ! Many of the pictured examples show variations on the technique ... e.g the designer chose not to put perspective lines in the landscape. The starting point for all was the same ...... attending a workshop ... but the results took many different routes to completion.

Patchwork patterns can be combined with scenic views, either imaginary or real. The perspective and colours flow from one to the other, blending or contrasting, enhancing both. All are machine sewn for speed and efficiency.

Perhaps the very best news of all is ......... that the techniques involved are easy to learn and apply. No artistic experience or special skill is required for design or sewing success ....... and nothing builds confidence like success. Beginners and experienced patchworkers alike can add a new design direction and a few new needlework tricks to their repertoire.

The degree of complexity in a project can also be varied. This will govern the time needed to complete the construction process. Again the choice lies with you .... a fast, simple landscape can be created omitting the patchwork surround ......
or alternatively the design chosen for the surround can be simple or detailed.
So get going .... plan and sew the heirlooms of tomorrow ...... whilst having fun, making and enjoying the finished product today.

## Before we Start.

*Here are some general points which will make life easier while you are sewing perspective scenes.*

1. **Freezer paper is essential to the techniques in this book.**  If you are unfamiliar with this type of paper ... it is useful because it sticks to fabric when ironed, shiny side down  .... but is easily removed, leaving no residue. It therefore makes great templates, and when bought it is blank, ready for you to draw on the dull side.
It is widely available in U.S.A.  in supermarkets by the roll as a cheap food wrap. This is the best source, so stock up if you are there on holiday. It can be bought more expensively in most quilt shops and mail ordered through 'Lakeland Plastics'.

It is used as the outer wrappers for many, *but not all,* packets of photocopying paper. ( Be nice to office workers for a free supply !) Open the packets carefully, so as not to tear them; cut away all glue spots as they will damage your fabric. Check to make sure it sticks to fabric before commencing designing on the dull side. These wrappers usually carry printing, so felt pen may be  required to clarify your design lines. The wrapper size is more limiting than purchased rolls.

2.  **Spray starch all fabric before starting work** ... making  it easier  to handle, especially washed, or hand dyed fabric, which has lost its 'crispness.' Starch will add stiffness for just as long as it is required. Handling  swiftly restores softness and drape. Pieced designs also benefit from a light starching. Always spray and iron on the wrong side, as over- enthusiasm might cause fabric  to become shiny.

3. **Use long, thin pins.**   They make such a difference when aligning fabric pieces for this technique. I personally like the type with the flat 'daisy'  shaped heads.

4.  **Iron seams as you work** ... have  your ironing board near at all times. This makes a great difference to the degree of accuracy achieved. The extra time taken is well spent, as you will probably be looking at the finished result for a long time. One good quality item is worth two roughly matched ones, pieced in the same amount of time. I keep a small ironing board and travelling iron on the table beside me as I work. This is more convenient than having to keep going to the full sized board. (Although that would be good exercise !)
The practice of peeling off the freezer paper shapes and re- ironing them over the seam allowance, as described in the text, is an **essential**  aid to accuracy.

5. **Use your rotary cutter with precision** ... many patchworkers do not ! (see p 45.)

6. **Stock up on size 60 machine needles.**   They have thin shanks  so make small holes. They do a great job on the curved seam technique described. However, they are inclined to break easily, so are not recommended for utility sewing.

7. **Check  that your roll of clear sticky tape will withstand the heat of an iron** ....
some melt .............. and it won't tell you that on the packaging !

# An Historic Perspective.

When comparisons are made between the art of different cultures and historical periods, it soon becomes apparent that there have been various approaches to representing the illusion of distance on a flat surface. The paper, canvas or wall on which pictures are painted has only two dimensions .... width and length. The reproduction of objects existing in space calls for greater ingenuity than simply painting a likeness. Primitive art ignored distance altogether. Everything was presented as being flat.

Early Eastern art showed figures which were all the same size regardless of their relative position. Where Western influence can be discerned, figures were often haphazardly smaller in the background, but there was no standard system.

Ancient Egyptians represented their world by changing the size of figures in accordance with their perceived importance and status in society, not their relative position in space.

The ancient Greeks were the first to explore the problem of depicting objects receding into the distance. In the sixth century B.C. they understood some basic perspective principles, and by the next century they were using aerial views showing shadows on the ground. They were interested in reproducing images to create the illusions of 3-dimensional buildings in painted stage scenery. The Romans also used colour variations to create the illusion of depth.

In the West the use of even rudimentary perspective was then ignored for many hundreds of years, until its thirteenth century revival in Italy. Leon Battista Albertini ( 1404 - 72 ) was the first to formalise a perspective system known as the 'Costuzione legittima' based on a pavement grid of perspective squares, as a formal linear framework. Using this grid artists were able to calculate the size of objects and people, using these appropriate dimensions, to create the appearance of distance on a flat canvas. This approach was correct but technically difficult to apply.

Leonardo da Vinci's genius allowed him to explore the implications of perspective in relation to the observed world. He was the first to examine the anomalies of depicting wide angled views, where apparently straight lines become curved at the perimeters of our vision. The subsequent study of perspective became ever more sophisticated, until the total abandonment of realistic painting at the end of the nineteenth century. We have grown used to modern painters deliberately distorting perspective to alter shape and space. Many today would deny the existence of any governing rules at all.

We are lucky that we can study all that has gone before, selecting the parts which might be of use to us as patchworkers. We can also be free enough to ignore the rest ...............
Don't forget to credit Leonardo's input to your next great quilt design !!

# Perspective for Patchwork.

There are many books on the subject of perspective, written for those who wish to work in the medium of paint. Patchworkers interested in widening their understanding of this fascinating subject may also find them helpful. However, a quick glance inside one of them may be daunting to many wishing to transfer these principles directly into the medium of fabric. It is not possible to apply exactly the same rules which govern painting. The unique problem of joining intersecting seams needs to be taken into account.

Patchworkers and painters have different requirements. It is therefore useful to understand how perspective principles work in general, then, where possible to modify them to suit our particular needs and constraints. (If Michelangelo had to assemble the Sistine Chapel ceiling by stitching sections together, he might have chosen to work by different perspective rules !)

'Perspective' is a system of creating the illusion of three dimensions in objects and patterns reproduced on a two dimensional surface, such as paper or fabric. Traditional patchwork patterns are mainly two dimensional, having width and length ..... quilting gives them a little height. This is not to detract from their lasting appeal. However, it is easy to give patterns a new lease of life, changing a flat appearance into one which provides the additional illusion of real depth.

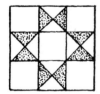  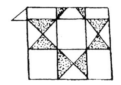 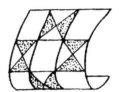

**Line** ......... can be used to create this feeling of depth by distorting a flat traditional patchwork block from the way we usually see it .....i.e. face on ....... and making it appear to lie down, fold or curl up. Our eyes are then fooled into believing that one part is nearer to us in space than the others, even though our brains tell us that this cannot be so. The use of lines in this way is called 'linear perspective' and is related to their position and length.

**Colour** ....... can further enhance this illusion of depth. We are often unaware at a conscious level that our brains are constantly interpreting colour information. No colour can be seen without light..... a rose is not seen as red in the dark. It is therefore easy to understand how our primitive ancestors believed the gods removed all colour from our world every night, returning it as a gift every morning. They were terrified if an eclipse darkened the day. The atmospheric effect of light and air changes our views of the landscape ... e.g. the colour tones of distant hills. Shadows, by their colour, position and length also affect our interpretation of what we see. The reproduction of these colour effects is called 'aerial' or 'atmospheric' perspective.

Linear perspective exploits the phenomenon that distant objects appear smaller to the eye. This is reinforced every day from our surroundings. We know that both railway lines and the sleepers between them appear to get progressively closer as they travel away from us. If parallel lines in a patchwork pattern behave in the same way, with space between them diminishing, our brain is convinced that they must be moving away from us into the distance. This effect is called 'foreshortening'.

We expect the space between parallel lines to reduce progressively as they travel away from us, and finally totally disappear as these 'vanishing lines' converge on the horizon at the 'vanishing point'. The vanishing lines help to determine the comparative size of distant objects and distance to the horizon.

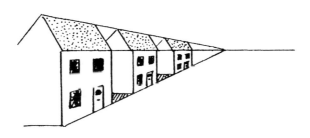

The viewer's eye is called the 'point of sight' ..... the line which represents the horizon is 'eye level'. The horizon is not a fixed line but is determined by the limit of the viewer's vision. It is most clearly seen when you look out to sea and nothing breaks the imaginary line separating sea from sky. If the horizon is unbroken it gives the impression of great space and emptiness.

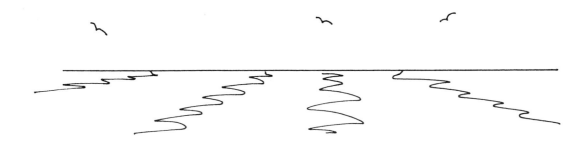

The position of the horizon can also vary. The higher your eye level ......
e.g. if you climbed to the top of a mountain ....... the higher the horizon would
appear. You would see more ground, or floor ......... and less sky or ceiling.

If your eye level is low ..... the opposite happens ... e.g. if you lie on your stomach
on the ground ...... you would see more sky or ceiling and less ground or floor. If
sky or land occupies the larger area in a picture, it has the greater emphasis placed
on it. If the horizon lies in the middle, equal emphasis is placed on both.

The placement of objects in a picture can also create different impressions of
depth .... e.g. A large area of background space is created by placing a tree in the
foreground and vice versa.

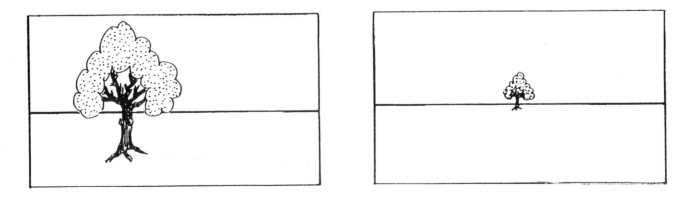

Objects will appear to lie above or below the horizon according to the height of your eye level.

If the nearest in a series of similar sized objects ....... e.g. trees, is seen as being positioned lower than the horizon ........ the remainder of the series will also be lower .... and vise versa.

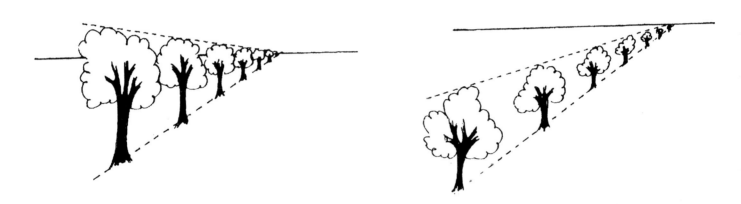

It is, of course, possible to create a picture containing only sky or land. If we depict a view which looks straight upwards into the sky there will be no land. Alternatively, looking down from a high standpoint, the land beneath us will contain no sky. This type of perspective is called 'bird's eye' perspective.

The effect of depth can also be increased by allowing one object or feature to overlap another. If we see this in a picture we judge that they must be at different distances from us. We assume that the one which is partially covered is further away and therefore behind the one in full outline. In this way several layers of overlapping hills can create an illusion of great distance.

The placing of objects ... e.g. vegetation, in the foreground creates a greater feeling of involvement for the viewer. We can see that it grows near to where we are positioned as we survey the scene. Being close, its size and detail will need to be greater than that of any other vegetation placed further away .... and our eye will estimate distance by comparison between the two.

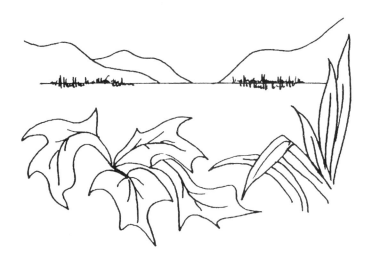

These rules for creating a three dimensional appearance in flat pictures should be used as helpful guidelines only, not as commandments. Perspective can be difficult to grasp for those who do not have both a mathematical and visual mind. (Even an acclaimed painter such as Edgar Degas hired a 'perspective adviser' to assist him.)

Further complications arise from the fact that we are able to see with two eyes .... each in a different position .... at the same time whilst our brain constantly merges both images into one, for interpretation.

Not only are we seeing two slightly different angles of an object at once, but we can also constantly move our heads from side to side and our bodies into different viewing positions.

Some Renaissance painters solved this dilemma by marking a fixed spot on the ground, from which their pictures were to be viewed, to obtain the full effect of their perspective efforts...... Just imagine this becoming the 'norm' at quilt shows!

> There are further perspective rules, but we are going to ignore them !!
> The following technique is easy to understand and apply ...
> it owes more to having fun and speeding the design process
> than to recreating the Renaissance.

Bearing in mind the preceding guidelines, there is just one last thing to remember when preparing to design your quilt ....

All four edges of the quilt are the parts which are nearest to you in terms of the three dimensional illusion. The top is the nearest part of the sky, whilst the base and sides are the nearest parts of the land.

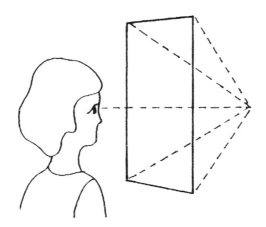

Perspective will create the impression that towards the middle of the quilt everything is getting further and further away from you, until the horizon is reached. This is therefore the most distant point in the illusionary scene.

**Now let's see how this illusion can be achieved ........ by the easy route !**

## The 'Easy Perspective' Design Process.

This technique requires no artistic skill of any kind, just the ability to remember the simple stages and to draw straight lines accurately, with the aid of a ruler.

For your first attempt, it is best to draft on scrap paper. The 'real' designs that you will complete later can be very much larger, (when you understand the system) and should be drafted on the dull side of freezer paper to facilitate the assembly technique.

### Drafting requirements.

1. A mechanical pencil ... the lead stays sharp and at a constant width.
2. A soft eraser.
3. Scrap paper for practice ........... Freezer paper for the real thing.
4. A ruler _**with a printed measurement grid**_ ... Long rulers, short rulers and quilter's squares can be useful at different stages depending upon the size of the design.

There is great value is practising the drafting of small scale designs .........
(ignoring the fact that they would contain impossibly minute pieces to sew together ) ...... you will quickly become familiar with the stages of the procedure. Let's try a practice run. We can look at the consequences and wider possibilities afterwards.

### Method.

1. Draw the outside shape of the design first. This is the design size without a border. Make it square or rectangular. For practice I recommend that these designs have sides of between 6 - 10 ins. **Do not** include fractions of an inch.

2. Calibrate all sides at 1 in. intervals, marking the corners A B C D as shown

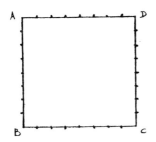
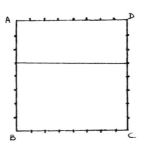

3. Mark the horizon by joining two matching side calibrations on A B and D C. For maximum effect place this line in the top half of the design thus creating a large floor area for pattern alternatives. Horizons placed in the lower half of the design cause distortions in the finished grid. ( See p 15. )

4. Locate the position of the viewer, by linking a matching top and bottom calibration on A D and B C ......... somewhere near the middle of the shape. (Positioning this line too near A B or D C results in a wall section too narrow to be useful. However, an off centre line adds interest). This line crosses the horizon at right angles. The crossing point is the vanishing point for all grid lines, and the focal point of the viewer.

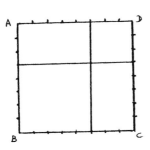
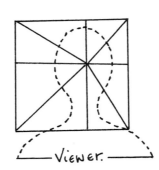
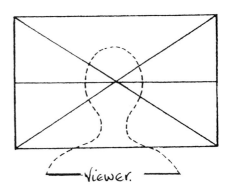

5. Join the focal point to all four corners A B C D of the outside shape. This will outline the ceiling, floor, and wall sections of the design.

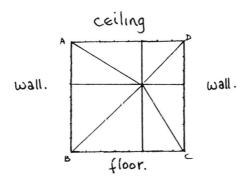

6. Draw the smaller inside shape which will contain the landscape. This can be any shape and must enclose the focal point. For practice make it either a square or rectangle.

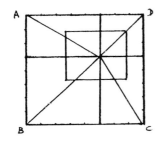
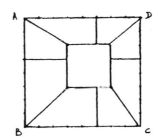
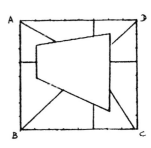

If this shape coincides exactly with the grid sections, the landscape is viewed as if through a window. If not, it appears more like a picture or cinema screen which has been placed in front of the grid.

7. Join the focal point to all the outside calibrations on the floor and ceiling sections only, on lines  A D  and B C.  This creates radiating vanishing lines on which we can construct a tiled grid for the patchwork blocks. *Do not*  draw the radiating lines on the wall sections yet as they  can look confusing at this stage.

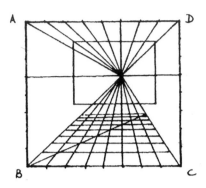

8. To draft the tiled floor grid correctly it is necessary to remind ourselves of the distance between the calibrations on lines A B C D ....... in the case of the practice run it was 1 in. Whatever it is in other sized designs, it will always be the width of the front row tiles. Create a point E. by marking the vanishing line *one removed from*  corner B, in the floor  section, at a point equal to the tile width, ( 1 in.) away from line B C.

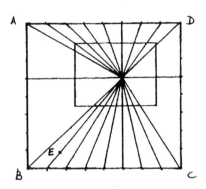

9.  Aligning corner B. with point E. lightly rule a diagonal line *across the floor section only* ............. *Do not*  ....... draw into the wall space on either side. This line will not be part of the tiled grid. It  is a light guideline only.

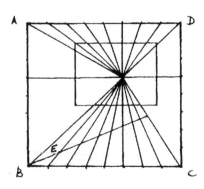

14

10. At the point where this diagonal crosses each vanishing line in turn, draw a horizontal line running parallel to line B C *across the floor only.* This will create the tiled grid. *Do not* ...... draw into wall spaces or inside landscape shape.

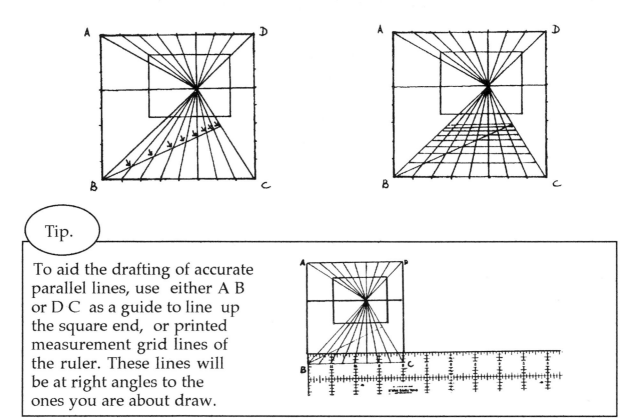

Tip.

To aid the drafting of accurate parallel lines, use either A B or D C as a guide to line up the square end, or printed measurement grid lines of the ruler. These lines will be at right angles to the ones you are about draw.

11. In the wall spaces on either side of the floor, draw vertical lines starting from the ends of each floor horizontal. Draft these lines upward, they must be exactly parallel to A B and D C ............ *stop at the edges of the ceiling.* Once again ...... *do not* ............ draw inside the landscape space.

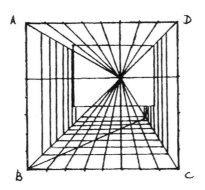

(These horizontal and vertical lines will create tiles which are elongated if the focal point is placed too close to the top, bottom, or either side of ABCD.)

If there is an area between the base of the central shape and the top of the floor tiles ....... do not worry. It can be treated as one piece of fabric for assembly purposes, with quilted vanishing lines and will look fine.

12.   Draw horizontal lines across the ceiling, which join the tops of the wall verticals. These horizontals will be parallel to line A D .... ( if you have been accurate) and will create the patchwork grid across the ceiling section.
Once again ....... **do not** ........ draw inside the landscape shape.

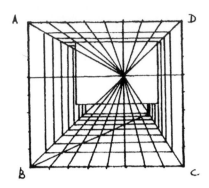

13.  Finally, draw the vanishing lines in both wall sections, from the focal point to each calibration on lines A B and C D.
The tiled grid is now complete. The inside shape also contains all the vanishing lines necessary to carry the perspective effect into the landscape.

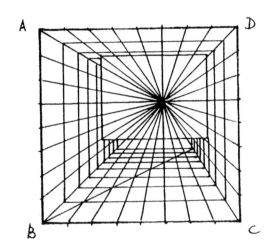 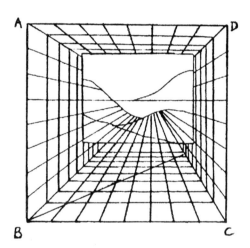

The novel insertion of scenery into a framework of perspective patchwork blocks is successful in this technique because the 'trompe l'oeil' effect of distance continues from one to the other without a break. One set of vanishing lines provides the framework for both. Patchwork designs are inserted into the tiled grid and the landscape superimposed on the same lines as they continue towards the horizon.
The landscape can be designed once the grid is in place. A final choice of pattern for the tiles can wait until the landscape is completed so that the relationship between the two can be clearly evaluated.
Designs such as these are ideal if used as wallhangings, or they can easily be drafted to any size. Create large sheets of freezer paper by clear taping several widths together, on the dull side. A really large design could fill a king size quilt top. A smaller one could provide an interesting central medallion in a quilt, if the size were to be increased by the addition of plain or decorative borders.

# Patchwork Possibilities.

1. All designs created by this method are made up of easily identifiable sections.

a. **The perspective patchwork section** ........ the tiled grid where the patchwork design will fit. The shape of this area can be varied. It may entirely surround the landscape, or sit against only a part of it.

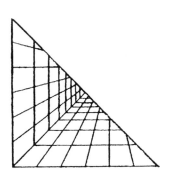
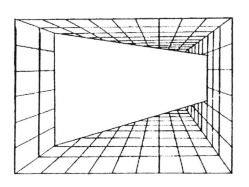
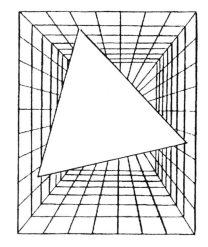

b. **The scenic landscape** .... this may take up as much as half the finished design area. It can be contained within a shape surrounded by patchwork, or may partly extend to the outside edge of the completed design. The perspective lines established in the patchwork pattern are echoed in the landscape to increase the effect of distance. These may be seams or quilting lines in the finished quilt.

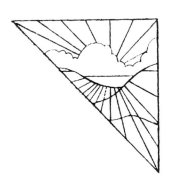
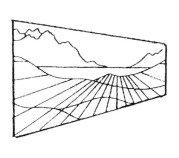
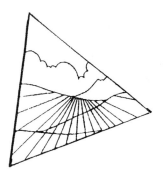

2. The choice of geometric pattern selected for the patchwork section really needs to be considered before the drafting begins. It will control the length of the sides of the outside shape. We know that traditional quilt blocks are of uniform size and square when examined 'face on'. The dimensions of a quilt are therefore calculated by multiplying the length of the side of a block by the number of times it repeats, (adding sashing and borders if applicable.)

In perspective quilts we want the blocks to appear as if they are receding into the distance. To achieve this effect, the lengths of the sides will now have to vary in every single block according to its position in the quilt.

The row of tiles at the front ... i.e. the base of the design, will be the largest. In the illusion they appear to be nearest to us. Each row 'behind' these will get progressively shorter in length, due to the effect of foreshortening. The lines forming the sides of the tiles also move closer together as they near the horizon, because they are vanishing lines.

The resulting effect on the framework of tiles is, that nearing the horizon they diminish in size and may well end up too small to be useful. The length of the sides in the front row of tiles is therefore crucial. This needs to be long enough to allow for the foreshortening effect to fall within usable limits ...........

**( For practice designs, I use between 1in. and 2ins, whilst for the 'real thing' I like to use side lengths of between three and six inches, depending on the size of the finished item)**

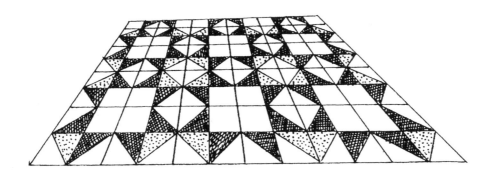

3. The tiled grid is our framework for constructing the chosen patchwork **pattern**. Each individual tile can be used to represent one part of a block. Thus **four** would make a 'four patch' and nine a 'nine patch' and so on.

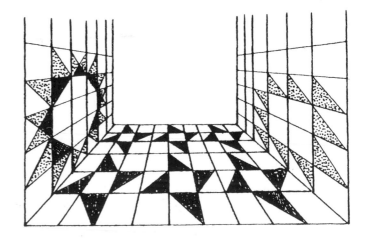

4. The floor section looks best if it is constructed from complete blocks. To achieve this the number of tiles across the front row would need to be a multiple of the chosen block format. (Your practice design may not have allowed for this).

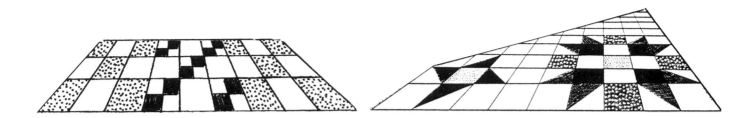

5.  The patchwork pattern can be chosen from many alternatives. This is a fun area in which to experiment and put your own individual stamp on a project.
This is also the area which can be altered to suit time requirements. Some patterns will take less time to complete, having less seam lines, or tiles can be 'merged' together to form larger sections, again cutting down on the number of seams.

> *There is very little difference in the degree of expertise required to sew one pattern as opposed to another, so do not be falsely restricted by misconceptions in that area. .... All seams are simply straight stitching.*

Choose from ....

a.  An all over pattern  ....  chequer board, random square,  or watercolour effect.

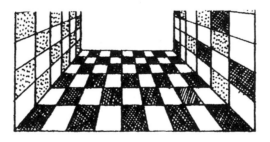

b. A single traditional style block surrounded by a 'background' pattern.

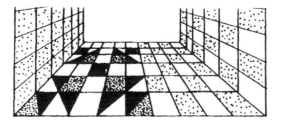

c. Traditional blocks combined to form all over patterns ...

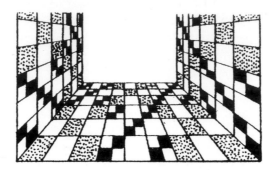

d. Traditional blocks alternating with wholecloth blocks.

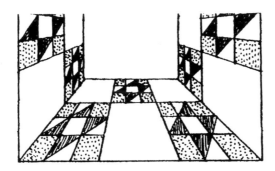

e. Traditional blocks spaced by  sashing,  ( one tile wide ).

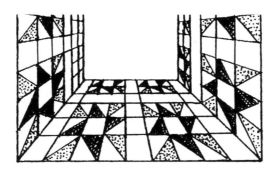

f. Combinations of the above.

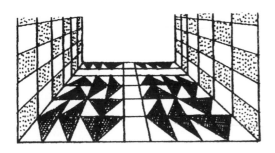 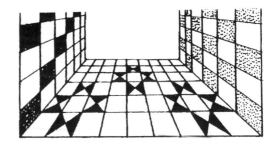

g.   Certain individual tile patterns lend themselves to the production of many original design combinations, and wonderful creative opportunities, especially when you add the magic ingredient ..... *colour*.

Small practice designs are great to colour, and open your mind to the endless possibilities. Half square triangles alone could keep you going for years !

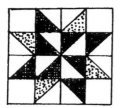 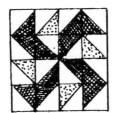 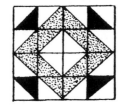 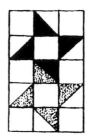

Using  half tiles makes for easy subdivisions for pattern alternatives. Using other part tile combinations can become a little confusing  to draft in a regular way as the tiles continually change shape.

However, do not be put off by this, as it is extremely satisfying for the more adventurous designer.

e.g. 'Storm at Sea'

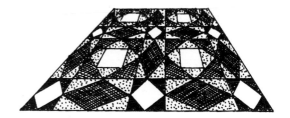

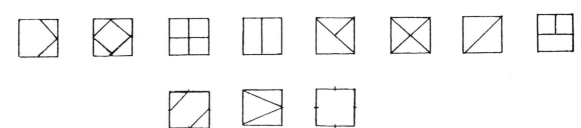

The above are simple, effective ways of dividing tiles. They are based on using the corners and mid-points of the sides as guides.

# Suitable Block Patterns to Choose From .....

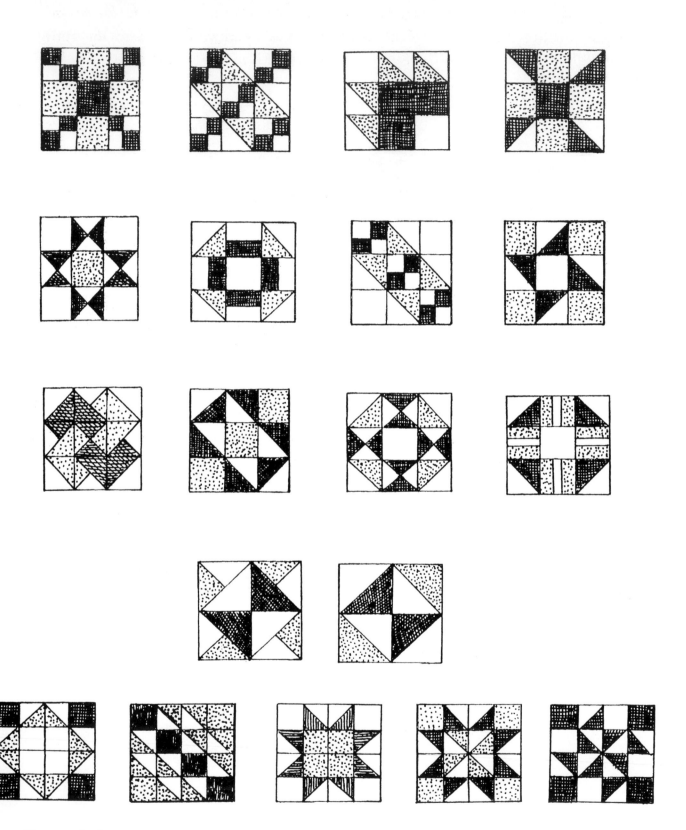

Do not feel restricted to these options ... they are presented as examples only. Try out ( at least on paper) any block that takes your fancy!

# Curving the Patchwork.

*(This section is an extension of the preceding ideas. You may wish to skip it for the moment and start reading again at page 27. Do however, look at the diagrams for some really exciting possibilities, and return when you understand the whole technique.)*

Easy perspective patchwork can take on a whole new look if the tiled grid is curved. The patchwork looks like a quilt waving in the breeze, or the landscape as if it were viewed from a magic carpet ride.

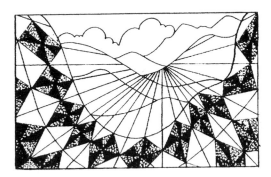 

This is just as easy to design and sew as straight patchwork, if the curves are all 'Tangential curves' ........ i.e. they are made up from straight lines ....... the curve is just another illusion. This is also useful from the stitching point of view, as the assembly process needs no particular expertise as it is all straight sewing.

Method.

The following instructions will draft a grid which links to the landscape on three sides.

 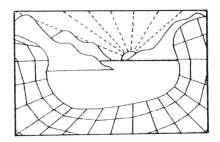

Again, for practice make it a small square or rectangle, drawn on scrap paper .......... The real ones will be larger and drawn on freezer paper.

1. Draw the required outside shape. Mark the corners ABCD as before.

2. Calibrate all sides of the shape, at regular, measured intervals. (In practice designs make it every inch.) Curved designs do not need a complete number of blocks in the floor area. It is not a clearly defined section in these designs.

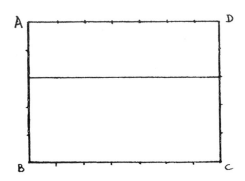

3. Mark the horizon by joining two matching side calibrations, in the top half of the shape.

4. Find the focal point by linking a matching top and bottom calibration with a vertical line, E F. Since there will be no wall vertical lines in this version, placing this line near sidelines AB and DC will not cause the development of tiny unusable tiles.

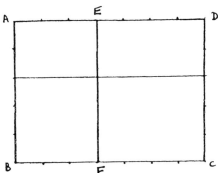

5. Draw a curving line, which will separate the landscape from the patchwork. This is the equivalent of the inside shape in the previous instructions. The exact starting and finishing points of this line are optional. The relationship of patchwork to landscape can have many variations, some are illustrated below.
( Be sure to make the curves large and gently sweeping .... not small and bumpy. )

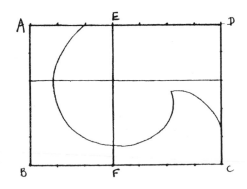

6. Join the focal point to all the side calibrations, creating the vanishing lines.

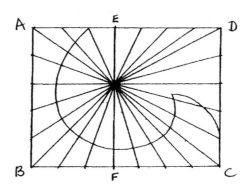

7. In curved designs the effect of foreshortening is achieved by drafting the tiled grid from the back forward. .... i.e. from the curved line to the base of the design. As the tiles are drafted they will increase in size towards the front.

This time it is not possible to use a diagonal to provide the reference points for the horizontal lines. Instead, the spaces on either side of the vertical EF, where it crosses the curved line, will provide our first measurement.

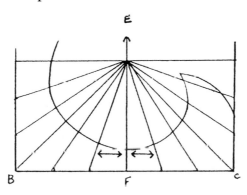

In most designs these spaces are different widths. Measure the wider space, rounding it up to the nearest easily usable measurement. It is best to use easily repeatable calibrations on the ruler ( e.g. 1/8 ... 1/4 ... 1/2 ... 1 in. etc.)

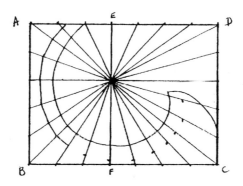

8. Starting from the curved line and measuring into the patchwork foreground, mark all vanishing lines at the above measurement. Join adjacent marks with short ruled lines. Although all these lines are *straight*.... (therefore easy to sew) .... they will echo the curve around the design, forming the back row tiles.

9. The next row of tiles will have to be bigger than the last. The vanishing lines are widening as they move forward  increasing the width of the tiles. The length can be increased by adding a little extra to the previous measurement.

e.g.  In a larger design where the measurement might be 3ins. the extra addition could be 1/4 in.             ..... or ....

In a practice design the measurement might be 1/2 in. and the extra addition might be 1/8 in.

Do not get obsessional when deciding exactly how much to add .....
a little  practice will give you confidence in your judgment ...
and no one is going to measure it and tell you that you were wrong !!
As long as the principle is followed it always looks convincing.

10. Place another mark on all vanishing lines in the patchwork section, at the previous measurement  plus the  additional amount. Join these marks as before.

Sometimes the marks will fall outside the design. These exterior dots will be necessary for the correct alignment of lines forming incomplete tiles in the grid.

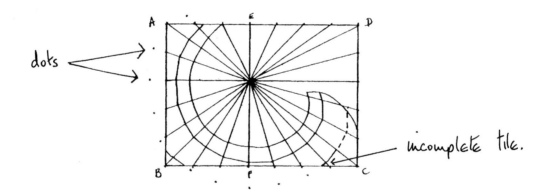

11. Repeat, adding rows of tiles, each at the previous measurement plus the same additional amount until the patchwork section is completed. Some vanishing lines will have more marks on than others, depending on the curve. The last  measurement marks may have to be placed outside the perimeter of the design in order to finish the last tiles which may not be complete.

The tiled grid in these curved designs is not absolutely correct in terms of accurate perspective. Don't worry about it ...... the designs will look great, and if distortion was good enough for Picasso   ...... it's good enough for me !

Curved grids can be used in exactly the same way as straight grids when planning patchwork patterns. *They are just as easy to sew together.*

# Creating Perspective in Landscapes

Fabric lends itself beautifully to the creation of landscape designs for wallhangings and quilts. Such designs are easy to construct, with no difficult drafting or sewing techniques involved. They can also combine perfectly with patchwork blocks, producing quilts which can soothe or excite. It is also a really great way to capture forever the memory of a special place.

Landscapes fall into two categories as far as this technique is concerned .... they will be considered separately and are ..........

a.    Scenes from the imagination ....... and ....
b.    Real places, taken from photographs or other pictures.

Imaginary scenes are a good starting point, because all the elements within the picture can be controlled and altered to facilitate the construction process. Examining the factors involved will also give valuable pointers worth considering when selecting a suitable picture of a real location.

Method.

Perspective landscapes can be drafted as designs, with or without patchwork surrounds. Once again, valuable experience can be gained from doing practice designs on scrap paper, although the real designs to be completed in fabric must be drafted on freezer paper.
(Landscapes with surrounds ... the landscape shape has already been drawn and the vanishing lines are in place ... go to point 4)

**Landscapes without surrounds.**

1. Draw the outside shape to the required size ( A square or rectangle to start.) calibrating all sides at regular, equal intervals as before. ( p 12. )

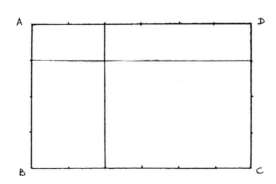

2. Draw the horizon and find the focal point by joining matching side and top calibrations as before.

3.  Link the focal point to all the side calibrations, thereby creating vanishing lines. The framework is now ready to have the landscape lines superimposed. This will create different sized and shaped sections suitable for patchwork.

4.  It is vital to consider piecing at this point, because this is where perspective rules which work for painters do not work for patchworkers. The problem arises at the vanishing point on the horizon.

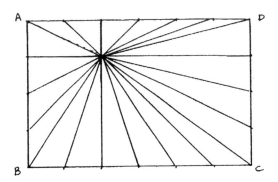

5.  It would not be possible to sew pieces of fabric together using lots of straight seams which all converge at the same vanishing point. This would create a major construction problem and result in an unsightly bump developing, from the accumulated seam allowances on the wrong side. As patchworkers, we would prefer to have a gap between each seam to prevent this happening and make life easier.

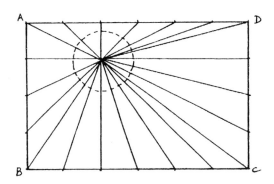

6.  We can create this ideal situation for ourselves if we bend the rules a little. Positioning the focal point *above* the horizon, *by moving the horizon line down* solves all our problems. Spaces are now created just where they are needed, between vanishing lines ... at the horizon.

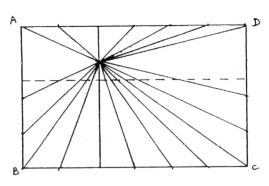

28

The easy way to do this is by drafting a landscape with a new horizon, placed lower than the previous straight line.  The vanishing point can then become the light source in the picture, with radiating lines which can be quilted across the sky, and patchworked across the land.

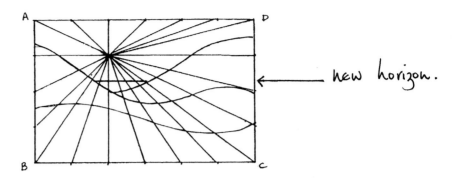

7.  If a flat horizon is required to suggest  e.g. a seascape or a desert,  draw a new straight horizon below and parallel to the first. The exact distance between them will vary according to the size of the design. The deciding factor will be the space you choose to  gain between vanishing lines  at the point this new line crosses them

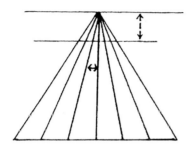 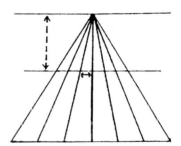

8.  Rolling hills are easy to include in your designs, creating an instant illusion of distance. Begin by drawing in the one which forms the new lowered horizon, adding others beneath it as follows .....
For drafting purposes,  hill lines  fall into three  categories,

a.  Lines which start on one side of the outside shape and  create a hill which extends across the  landscape finishing on the other side.

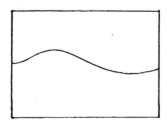

b.  Lines which start at one side of the outside shape and create a hill which ends by vanishing behind another. These lines do not reach as far as the other side.

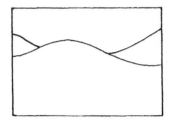

c.  Lines creating hills which both start and finish behind others. Neither end of these lines touches the sides of the outside shape.

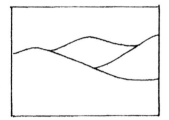     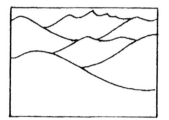

A combination of the above gives the most realistic impression.

9.  If an area of water .... e.g. a lake is required, this is most effectively drawn as a straight line.

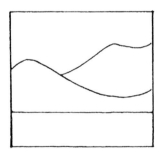     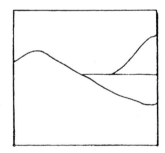

Wavy lines which are supposed to represent the far shore of the lake seldom look believable.

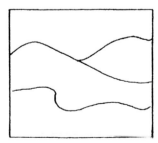     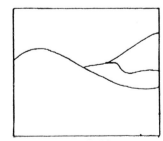

10  Erase the vanishing lines on the sky and water areas of the design. This clarifies the effect you are achieving.  (If you do require the lines across the sky as guides for quilting  the rays of the sun they can be added again later.)

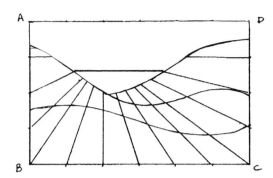

11. Lay out all landscape sections before considering additional features such as trees, vegetation and clouds. I usually draw them on pieces of scrap paper, cutting various sizes and shapes and trying them in different locations until I'm satisfied.  They can then be cut out in freezer paper.

The 'roots' of trees etc. can be inserted into the seams between the individual pieced sections of landscape as they are joined. Appliqué stitching around the remainder of the shape can be finished later.

I like the effect of vegetation 'escaping' from the landscape into the patchwork ... these pieces can be finished off last of all when landscape and patchwork sections have been joined.

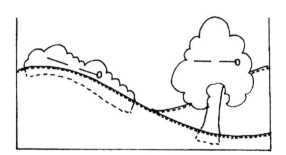
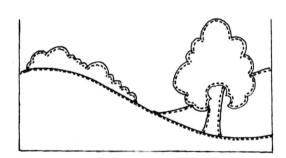

## Landscapes from reality.

The idea of depicting real scenes in these designs will appeal to many. Personal photographs, calendars, magazines and travel brochures all contain inspirational scenes just waiting to be used. ( Do however be mindful of copyright !)

This is another area in which the choice of fabric rather than paint as our medium will force the adoption of a different approach. We cannot represent fine detail, blend colours or achieve an exact copy of reality in quite the same way as paint. Fabric is more of a ' blunt instrument'. Fabric pictures are usually more stylised and simplified than paintings, with a character all of their own. This is not to say that they are inferior in any way ..... they are just different.

## Choosing the right picture.

Although in theory all pictures can be reproduced in fabric, some will be more suitable for this technique than others. Attempting to reproduce every little detail may create assembly problems. For this reason it is often a good idea to aim for an impression of the scene, rather than striving to produce an exact replica.

## Method.

a. The perspective effect achieved by the drafting of vanishing lines will be wasted if there is not a representation of distance in the photograph. Therefore avoid views in which distance cannot be observed.

b. The content of the picture will need to be simplified, enabling the main features to be drafted as straight and curved lines dividing the scene into sections which can be pieced, just as for imaginary scenes.
Taking a tracing of the most important features of the photograph can quickly clarify these main sections.

*Completing this tracing on transparent acetate, such as an overhead projector transparency , rather than tracing paper, has several advantages.*

- It is much easier to see the feature that you are tracing.
- If an appropriate non permanent felt pen is used, alternatives can be tried out or mistakes removed.
- The finished tracing can be photocopied, and therefore enlarged to a required size if you are not confident in your copying skills or want a quick result.
- lastly ......

> **Most Important of All** ....... the sewing technique described later causes the whole design to be _**reversed**_ as it is assembled. This does not matter if using an imaginary scene as no one will ever know.
> However, as you will not want reality to be reversed ......the transparent tracing can easily be flipped over. This enables a reverse copy to be made, and the sewing process will then restore the correct view.

**'Out of Africa.'** 33 x 25 ins. by Chris Graves
St. Albans. Herts

**'Spring has sprung !'**
24 x 24 ins.
By Shirley Winchester.
Harpenden. Herts.

'Aspect on Delft'.
31 x 29 ins.
By Jenny Hipperson.
Harpenden. Herts

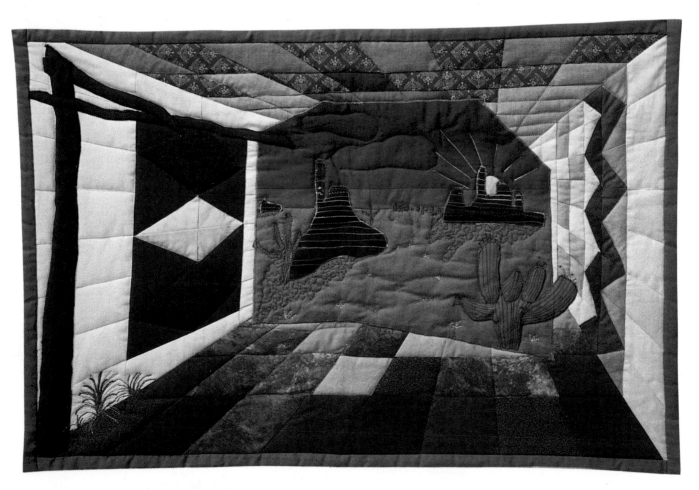

'Navajo Linoleum.'    20 x 30 ins.  by Nora Field. Hemel Hempstead. Herts.
(Inspiration taken from a travel brochure ... and so titled after an elderly neighbour
admiring the wallhanging had asked " Do you know that your linoleum looks flat ?")

Above. **'Starry, Starry Night.'**
30 x 43 ins.
By Alison King.
St. Albans. Herts.

Below. **'Alpine Holiday'**
20 x 32 ins.
By Carmen Redler.
Hemel Hempstead.
Herts.

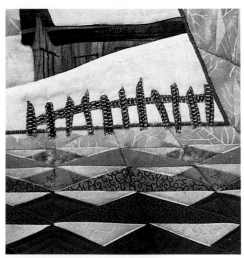

'Due South.'
24 x 24 ins.
(in pine frame)
By Judy Wilson.
Wheathampstead. Herts.

'Arran.'   13 x 20 ins. By Kathleen Mc. Mahon. Watford. Herts.

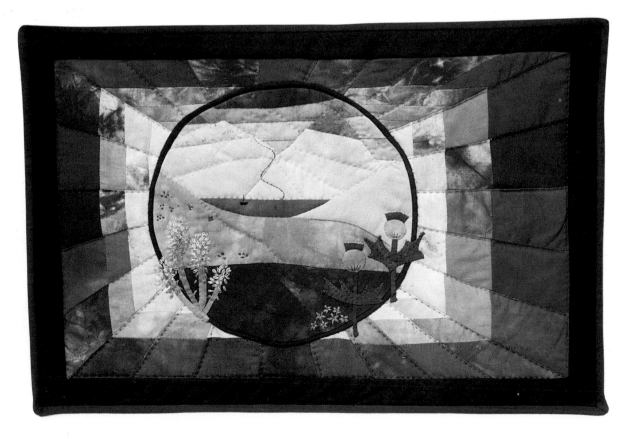

**'Poppies on Bluehouse Hill.'** 19 x 25 ins. by Sue Martin. Boxmoor. Herts.

**'Deeper Still.'** 43 ins. x 43 ins.
 By Sue Martin.Boxmoor.Herts.
(The landscape is a piece of printed fabric.)

**'Whale Song.'** 39 x 42 ins.
by Sue Martin. Boxmoor. Herts.

# Selecting the Right Fabric.

Now that the design is finished, the fun of translating it into fabric can begin. Selecting the right fabrics may be confusing if you are new to patchwork or doubt your ability in this area.

If we make another comparison with the art of painting ...... no one would suggest that an artist would set out to recreate a scene without a paint box containing a basic variety of colours. These could be mixed together to create even more different colours.

Patchworkers too need this variety of colours from which to select. In fact we need many more than an artist, as we cannot mix ours together. The more diverse your fabric collection becomes, the greater the chance of finding 'just the right piece'. It is not necessary to collect long lengths, as these designs use small pieces. Collect and add to your collection whenever you can. Buy 1/4 yd lengths ..... or more if you really fall in love with something which is extra special.

Beware of fabric that you consider 'too nice to cut up' .........we have all got those, ........ kept only to be stroked and admired ! The inevitable result of being kept too long is, that as tastes and fashions constantly change, ... today's wonderful fabric will look dated tomorrow .... so use it now while it gives you the most pleasure.

Make sure that you include colours which you do not naturally incline towards, especially those you might not choose to wear ... e.g. yellow. A full range of colours appears in the natural world. A little of the colour you avoid may be just what is needed. Use the wrong side of fabrics too; it's often a lighter version of the front.

It is also worthwhile collecting fabrics which are not usually considered to be patchwork fabrics ...... lurex ...... velvet ...... satin etc etc. These will add a little extra sparkle when combined with cotton and will not be difficult to work with as the freezer paper will keep them stable.

**Unsuitable Fabric.**

Fabrics which are stiff or thick will create bulky seams. Striped or squared patterns do not work for this technique as the uniform width of the stripe or the squares conflicts with the narrowing perspective of the tiled grid. Also remember that designs on patterned fabrics must diminish in size as the tiles recede into the distance if the illusion is to be believed.

**Colour ..... The essential ingredient that brings designs to life.**

Colour is a very personal matter; we all have our own views and requirements. We may want to match curtains or upholstery, create a mood, or brighten a dark corner ......... or just love working with blues!.

**Here are a few ideas which may help....**

a. Take a picture that you like ... possibly the one you have chosen to copy, or any other .... e.g. a postcard or advert ... you just like the effect of the colours it contains. Using one of the packets of tiny fabric samples from mail order fabric suppliers, match all the colours as nearly as you can. Try to be aware of the relationships and relative amounts of neighbouring colours ...... they may be more effective in combination than alone. Use these matched samples as your guide. The exact fabric may not be available, just look for something that's close.

( See p 70. the 'Connemara lily' wallhanging, ..... here the chosen colours were taken directly from the photograph that was copied ... with a little more sky blue added to brighten up the day !).

b. Look in quilt books and magazines to find a quilt that appeals. Use the same colours in your perspective blocks, carrying them into the main parts of the landscape. Extend the range by including several lighter shades and darker tones of the chosen colours.

c. Take your lead from Mother Nature. Decide on a season to be represented in the scene ..... continue appropriate seasonal colours into the patchwork.

d. All landscapes do not have to be completed in natural colours. Pick a colour not usually associated with scenery and use a range of that colour to complete the whole design ... e.g. pink.

e. Pick a special, patterned fabric to be used in the perspective block and echo the colours it contains in the rest of the design.

f. Take a closer look at nature ... check out geographic magazines, etc., and look more closely at the amazing colour combinations present in different parts of the world ... different species of animal .... flowers ..... shells ... butterflies, sky effects and underwater. Sharpen up your observation; it will encourage you to get more adventurous and build confidence.

g. Peek inside colour photography books in bookshops and libraries. Often the ordinary can become extraordinary by the use of coloured lens filters.These can be a wonderful source of inspiration. Some tourist postcards and greetings cards have been produced in this way, so check out the card stands if you're away.

h. Keep a file of pictures ... cards ... even wrapping paper that might be useful for future inspiration. A little time ignoring the overall effect (which is all we usually see) and homing in on the individual constituents which contribute in differing amounts to that effect, can teach us a lot.

i. Make multiple photocopies of a design. Colour each one differently and compare the result. They are often surprising. Identical patchwork blocks look completely different with the strong colour placed in varied positions.

j.  Whatever the colour scheme you finally decide upon, remember that the effect of distance, created by the linear perspective grid, will be increased and enhanced if you follow the aerial perspective colour rules .............

    a.  The base of the quilt should have the strongest and brightest colours, as it is nearest to you in the illusion.

    b.  Land colours should pale as they move up the quilt and be at their palest at the horizon.

    c.  The sky fabrics should reverse that order, with the strongest colour placed at the top of the sky, where it is the nearest to being overhead, in the illusion.

There are many fabrics available today printed in varying gradations of the same colour ..... e.g. from navy ...... to the palest light blue. These are a valuable addition to your fabric stack and are ideal for suggesting aerial perspective.

Gradation dyeing can also produce ideal fabric colours.

---

**However** ..... do not put off trying this technique if you cannot find this ideal graded fabric. Remember that the perspective rules were only a guide. The use of linear perspective alone will guarantee some pretty special quilts.

---

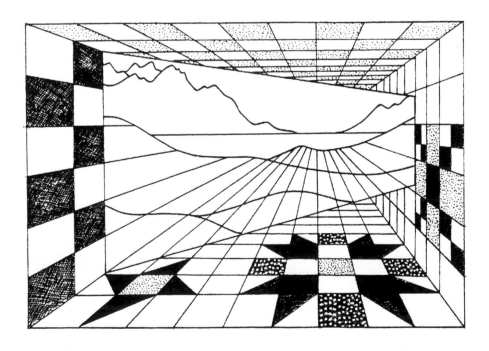

# *Speedy sky effects.*

It often seems easier to find fabric which will piece together to form the land sections of designs than to locate something ideal for the sky. Some commercial fabrics have been specially printed with cloud effects in different colours and increasing numbers of patchworkers now dye their own cloth. Either or both of these sources may provide exactly what you are looking for.

If the need has still not been met, consider spray painting to create the desired effect. It is faster and easier to control than using dye and very inexpensive. With a little practice it can produce a very professional result, and the colour does not fade if exposed to sunlight.

### Requirements.

Old newspapers.
Thin cardboard ... cereal packet or similar.
Scissors, or craft knife.
Car or bicycle spray paint in required colours.
Plain fabric.
Kitchen roll paper.
Face mask
A well ventilated area in which to spray.

### Warning

**As when using dyes, sensible precautions need to be taken to prevent the inhalation of the paint or propellant gas .... they are poisonous.
The wearing of a mask will prevent you breathing in the actual paint ... but not the propellant. Therefore it is unwise to use paint sprays in enclosed areas, where the fumes cannot escape.
Do not use sprays if you suffer from breathing difficulties or are pregnant.**

### Method.

1. Prepare a table surface, and, if necessary, protect the floor and nearby walls by covering them entirely with newspaper. If a well ventilated area is not available ........ go outside, if the weather permits and there is no wind.

2. Wash and iron the fabric, cutting it into appropriately sized pieces for your planned projects. The content of the fabric is irrelevant, but, of course, light colours are best to show up the paint effect. Experiment with different colours.

3. Cut different sized 'clouds ' from one edge of several pieces of cardboard with the knife, or scissors. These will be simple curved shapes, which can be drawn in advance, if you are not confident of designing as you cut.

You will be aiming the spray at the shaped edge, so make sure the cardboard piece is large enough to grasp along the straight edge. The card masks the area of fabric which represents the cloud. The paint produces the sky beyond. Using different sized clouds in combination will produce a more realistic effect.

### 4. **A few points when using paint sprays.**

a. Use at room temperature; they are less efficient when cold.

b. Do not expect the colour exactly to match the spray can lid .... The fabric surface and colour may change it slightly e.g. metallic paints no longer appear metallic. ( 'Luminous' yellows and pinks sold in bike shops are great for sunsets).

c. Always test the spray before use to make sure it works properly and does not make blobs. Once the colour is on the fabric ........... ( or anything else for that matter ........ so corral the cat !! ) ........ **it cannot be removed**

d. Spray a few test runs against your cardboard clouds, on paper, to make sure the shapes produced are to your liking.

e. Hold the card a short distance ... an inch or so ... above the fabric and aim the spray at the edge.This will create a soft diffused effect. The line produced becomes more defined the nearer the cardboard is held to the fabric.

f. Do not spray in long bursts ....... use short, quick, bursts which will spray the paint lightly. It is always possible to re-spray for a heavier effect

g. Combine colours for exciting effects. Try light blues, greys, pinks, yellows, reds and purples for wonderful, custom made sunsets. Alternatively, spray in colours to coordinate with the patchwork.

h. Spraying can also be used to change any fabric used in other parts of the quilt. Create original features e.g. vegetation or fields, by using stencils. Spray against a straight edge to suggest ploughed furrows, perspective lines etc.

> **Important tip.** As soon as each piece of fabric has been sprayed, submerge it in water. This will not affect the paint, which dries instantly, but will prevent the fabric from continuing to release propellant fumes. Spray painting does not make fabric stiff, once dried and ironed it is ready for use.

# From Paper to Quilt ... the Assembly Process.

Once the design is finished, and fabric selections have been made, the assembly process can begin. The two sections ... perspective patchwork and landscape ... are completed separately, then combined. Let us take the patchwork first ........

1. Pieces can be easily labelled if they are cut apart a few at a time. Number, and letter individually. A coloured line drawn through each wedge will help seams correctly register.

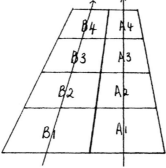

Individual sections can be sewn in manageable stages, pinned on a design wall or board, awaiting the completion of neighbouring sections. Remember that the whole design will be **_reversed_** when sewn.

2. Individual freezer paper shapes will be ironed, using a moderately hot iron ...

   ***shiny side down*** ....... onto .......... ***the wrong side*** **of the fabric.**

1/4 in seam allowances are added around each shape when cutting the fabric.

3. It is efficient and speedy to separately cut paper and fabric freehand, using a rotary cutter. The essential accuracy can be achieved with a little practice and confidence.

The idea of using a rotary cutter freehand without a ruler may seem daunting. It just takes a little practice and the correct grip on the cutter to achieve maximum accuracy. It is very much faster than using a scissors.

Having trained as an Occupational Therapist, I am aware that different hand grips affect the performance of everyday tasks. Embarking upon a new activity sometimes requires a little analysis and practice. Few would argue that it did not matter how you held chop sticks or a golf club for success.

Contrast the pincer grip you would choose to pick up a pin, with the barrel grip necessary to hold a tennis racquet.

   One is a ***precision grip,*** while the other is designed for ***power.***

A rotary cutter is designed to be a precision cutting tool, enabling patchworkers to cut fabric accurately. A precision grip is therefore the most appropriate choice.

The index finger of the dominant hand should be extended and placed on top of the cutter, just behind the blade. There is usually a serrated area on which to rest the pad of your finger. This is the most efficient grip when holding a knife, fork, or pen, providing maximum fine control.

*Try holding the above tools with the same grip as you would choose for a tennis racquet. It is comfortable, but dramatically lessens the degree of fine control it is possible to exert when using the tool.*

The power necessary to cut through several layers of fabric at once can be maximised by holding the cutter in a reasonably vertical position ........
Downward pressure can then be exerted through your palm. The nearer the cutter handle is to the horizontal, the less power you will be able to apply. (This is crucial if the blade is less than razor sharp and is often the reason that sewers cut inaccurately, by accidentally swerving away from the ruler's edge ).

If this is new to you, the feeling of unfamiliarity rapidly declines with use.

Tip
It is interesting to try out different types of cutter, as the handle length and girth varies considerably. You may find one much more comfortable than others, and better suited to the size of your hand

4. If a major inaccuracy occurs when freehand cutting your paper, it can easily be repaired with clear tape, ready for another try. Minor inaccuracies will take care of themselves as the sliver accidentally cut too wide on one side of the line will be stuck to the neighbouring piece on the other side of the line !.... therefore ....

*As shapes are always sewn to their immediate neighbours ... they ALWAYS fit.*

5. The floor of the patchwork section is a good place to start cutting the tiles apart. If they are cut into strips, along the vanishing lines from the base of the quilt towards the landscape, individual pieces are conveniently placed to position fabric colours so they become paler as they are positioned higher on the strip, for the aerial perspective. Cut one strip at a time.

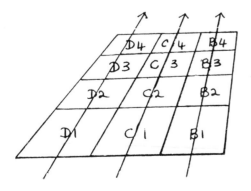

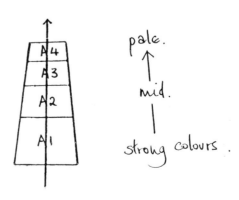

6. Iron all paper templates to fabric allowing a generous 1/2 in. between them. Rotary cut each piece freehand with at least 1/4 in. seam allowance.

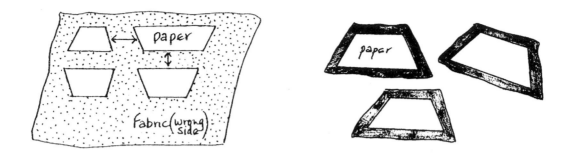

7. Individual tiles are reassembled if they contain a block pattern and then sewn together to reform the strip. Completed strips can be joined along the vanishing lines to remake the floor section. If all vanishing lines are unbroken seams they will be straight and enhance the perspective effect.

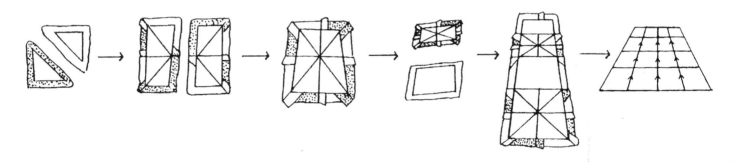

8. The positioning of the paper templates on fabric does not have to follow the straight grain. The paper remains stuck to the fabric throughout the construction process, providing stability and preventing distortion. This also facilitates a very economic use of fabric, as many shapes can utilise small scraps.
If, however, it is important to have everything on the straight grain, this is easy to achieve, if the letters or numbers used for labelling are carefully written so that they all face the same way, they can then be used as direction guides, to reinforce the coloured lines already mentioned.

9. In order for the finished quilt to have correctly matched seams throughout and also lie flat on completion, the cutting and sewing processes must be as accurate as possible. Drafting on freezer paper has produced very accurate templates which are (temporarily) secured to the fabric. The edges can now be used as clear sewing guides All stitching should fall beside, ....... not on top ... of the paper's edge.

10. It is helpful to develop the habit of laying out each row of fabric tiles, in their correct order, paper uppermost, prior to sewing. This prevents their being joined together incorrectly ... **and remember matching sides are always an exact fit.**

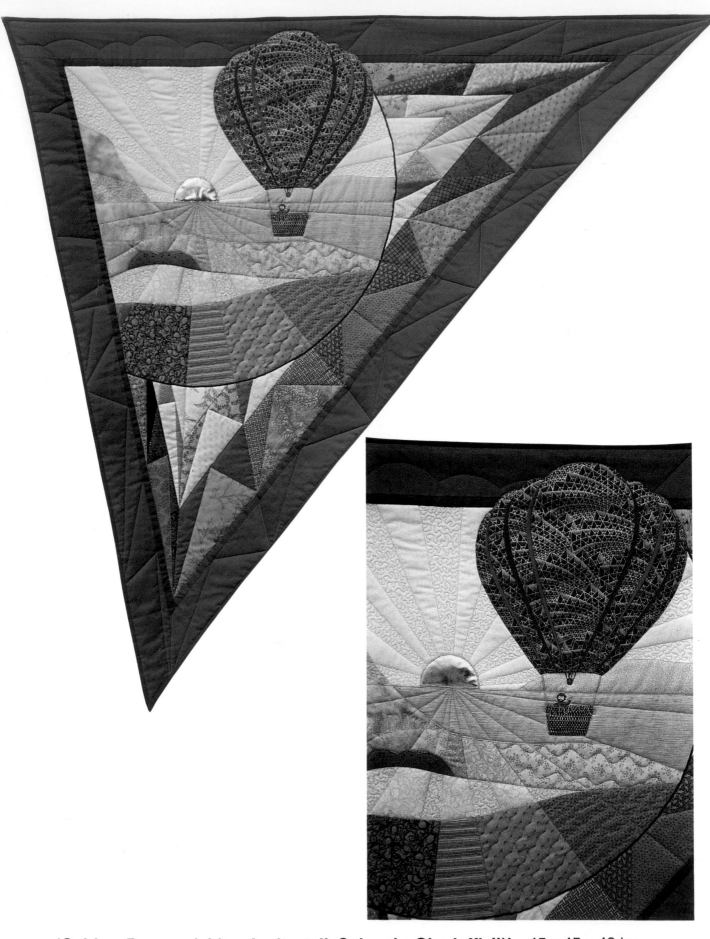

**'Golden Days ....(shh.. don't tell Colonel Ghadaffi !!)'** 45 x 45 x 49 ins.
By Sue Martin. Boxmoor. Herts.

Many different quilt shapes are possible using this technique ........The fact that they may not always have a floor, ceiling and walls alters the effect, but not the basic principle. Place calibrations around all sides of the varying outside shapes.

**'Terra Australis'**
28 x 32 ins.
By Denise Matthews.
Little Gaddesden.
Herts.
(& Australia.)

**'Pink Ice.'** 39 x 39ins. by Sue Martin. Boxmoor. Herts.

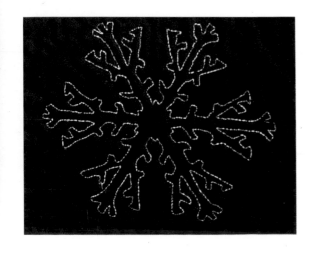

**'Laura Loves Sunsets.'** 46 x 55 ins. by Angela Madden.
(Six cord plaited border can be easily drafted using my 'Multi- plait tool')

**'Into the Dawn.'**   52 x 58 ins.   by Angela Madden.

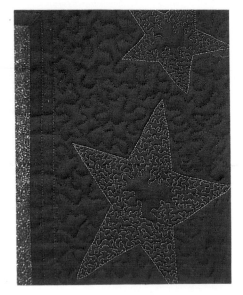

# Sewing Perfect Seams.

Sewing can be a very satisfying activity if it goes well and everything fits together just like a jig-saw puzzle. However problems at this stage will ruin the enjoyment, and the offending item often joins other unfinished projects in the back of the cupboard. Not this time !! ....

***The following techniques will ensure trouble free sewing.***

1. Starting at the base of the quilt, preparing to work up the row of the decreasing sized tiles towards the landscape, take the first two adjoining fabric floor tiles. Match them together with right sides facing, ready to pin the seam which is to be joined.

2. Insert a pin through the fabric on the first tile, from the wrong side, at one end of the freezer paper. ( Long, fine pins are best. )

3. Align the second tile behind the first, so that the point of the pin exits at the equivalent point to its entry.

4. Push half the length of the pin into the seam, leaving it sticking straight out.

5. Repeat with another pin at the other end of the paper.

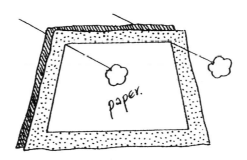

6. Depending on the length of the seam, it may be necessary to insert one or more pins between the previous two. These should be inserted at the paper's edge bringing both sides into precise alignment. Take care not to pin through the paper itself on either side.

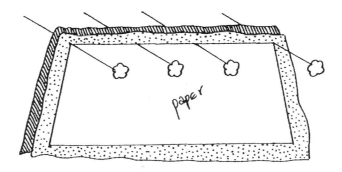

7. Re - insert the full length of the two outer pins, facing points inwards towards each other. Do this as if they were needles performing little 'running stitches' along the paper's edge. If additional pins have been used, face them all towards the left, running them along in the same manner.

I can achieve greater accuracy by completing each seam in two stages, starting to sew from part way along and continuing to one end, as follows .....

8. Begin to stitch the seam in the space between opposite facing pins, travelling along the paper's edge to the end of the fabric. Use a stitch length which is a compromise between being small enough to be secure .... and being large enough to be undone without much difficulty, should the need arise.

9. As you stitch, hold the head of the pin immediately in front of the needle. It will be extending towards you and is easy to grasp ....... Do not pull it out ....
hold it in a constant position, allowing it to be withdrawn gradually, as the fabric is moved away by the action of the machine.

The pin will continue to anchor the fabric in the correct position for as long as possible, just in front of the needle, but the needle will never hit the pin. Remove all pins in this way.

10. When the first stitching is complete, flip both tiles over to stitch the open end of the seam. Always oversew 1/4 in. of the previous stitching to lock the threads.

11. Trim any loose threads and the seam allowances to a neat 1/4 in. Also snip a diagonal cut across both ends of the seam allowance. This will reduce the bulk at intersections.

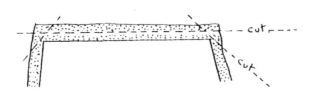

**Pressing the seams.**

After every seam has been sewn it is important to press it before continuing. For this purpose an iron and board are usefully positioned nearby. All seams should be pressed to one side, and wherever possible seams which will cross others should be pressed in opposite directions.

**Method.**

1.  On the completion of every seam,
    it should be pressed to the chosen side.

2. The Freezer paper should be lifted from
   underneath both allowances, allowing
   the fabric to be tucked underneath the
   paper template.

3.  Replace the freezer paper on top of
    the seam allowance, carefully iron it down
    *so that the edges of the papers meet exactly .*

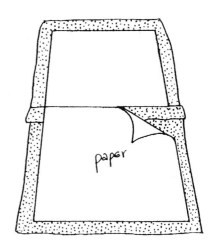

**Lifting and repositioning the paper is <u>essential</u> for accuracy .....
and helps in the following ways.....**

By holding the seam allowances firmly in the chosen direction

By firming up the design and making it easier to handle.
The seams between small sections of the design are stiffened so that they
behave like one large solid piece.

By highlighting slight discrepancies in alignment which may have occurred
during stitching. It is easy to reposition one or both papers to restore accuracy.
**Yes! ........ if it is not right move the paper!! ............ ( I won't tell anyone.)**

By keeping the design perfectly flat during the construction process.

By keeping all the construction markings and template edges clearly visible.

**Sewing patterns within a tile.**

At first glance it may seem a difficult job to continue block patterns into the smaller tiled areas of the patchwork. There is obviously a limit to the size most people would be prepared to tackle unless there is a great love of making miniatures. The great thing about this technique is that you can decide the level of complexity.

1. Clearly the easiest option of all is to cut the floor, ceiling and wall sections as one piece of fabric and ignore piecing altogether........ the perspective lines can be quilted or embroidered in place.

2. The next easiest option is to piece some sections and not others. The largest tiles are always in the floor so this could be pieced ...... but a narrow wall section, or the smallest tiles at the back of the floor could be cut as one solid piece.

3. Chequer boarding, random squares or watercolour effects are patterns which have no subdivisions within individual tiles, so are very straightforward to assemble.

4. Using one large pieced block set into background squares is also a quick and easy alternative to consider.

5. As individual tiles become too small to piece in the patchwork pattern .... replace them with a unpieced tile, which by choice of fabric gives the overall dark, medium, light shading expected of that tile.


**Strip piecing.**

The technique of strip piecing whereby fabric strips are sewn together, the seam is pressed flat and the newly formed stripped fabric is re-cut to form the pattern is a useful one to utilise. It can make handling very small sections much easier.

Consider the pattern "Ohio Star,"
where four subdivisions requiring diagonal
quarter square triangles are required. This
is an ideal pattern in which to use
strip piecing.

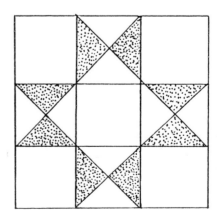

**(It is unnecessary to use this technique
for larger "Ohio Star"tiles as it is more
wasteful of fabric and the normal sewing
method will work well for these.)**

**Method.**

1.  The exact width of each strip required will depend upon the size of the design .... and will inevitably be an approximate measurement, as all the small sections containing these quarter square triangles will vary in size. Study the tiles targeted and choose one size strip which is wide enough to accommodate the widest triangles plus 2 x 1/4 in seam allowance.

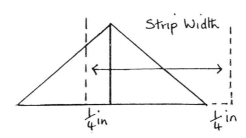

2.  Cut these strips in the two chosen colours. It is not possible to give exact length measurements as again this will also depend upon the design size.
Make a 'guesstimate'.

3.  Sew the strips together with 1/4 in. seam allowance. On completion, press both allowances towards the darker colour.

4.  Before cutting the tile into separate sections, check that you have labelled, and seam marked all the subdivisions of the tile. Highlight those which will contain the darker colour, with a coloured marker.

      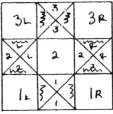

R. = Right

L. = Left.

3 = dark.

5.  Cut the tile into the nine squares. Cut the subdivided squares diagonally once only ..... this will leave two diagonal half square triangles still joined, in each triangular section.

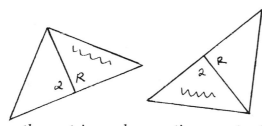 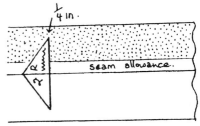

6.  Iron these triangular sections onto the wrong side of the stripped fabric, aligning the seam with the central marked line. Check that the dark fabric matches the marked triangle on the paper. The different shapes will lie in different positions according to their position in the block ....... but the seam will always align with the central line. Re-cut the fabric allowance around the paper.

# Stitching Diagonal seams.

Experienced patchworkers will know only too well the problems associated with the accurate joining of pieces where previously stitched seams cross on the diagonal.  The pieces can be lined up correctly with a pin piercing the crossing point ....... everything  seems fine until the pin is flipped over to secure the point prior to sewing ..... this action moves the fabric out of alignment and stitching secures the badly matched seam.

***Not any more ...***

Wherever these diagonal seams occur, this simple tip will dramatically increase your accuracy ... and save your temper !
The answer to the patchworker's prayer lies in the use of double sided sticky tape.

1.  Match the fabric pieces to be joined, right sides together, with a pin accurately through the crossing point of the seams. To double check accuracy, poke the pin through one piece checking its position on both sides of the fabric. It should be on on the stitching at the edge of the freezer paper on the wrong side and on ***the exact centre*** of the seam on the right. Next match that accuracy through the other piece. Leave the pin sticking straight out. If you are stitching a seam with lots of crossing   diagonals  place a pin  through every one.

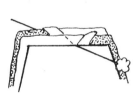 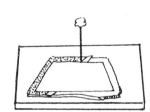 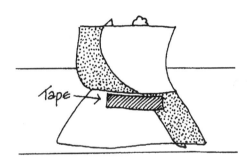

2. You will need a board that you can pin into .... ( I use the inside flat cardboard roll that fabric bolts are wrapped around ..... beg one from your nearest shop.) Lay the fabric on the board so that the pins can be stuck straight down into it at right angles to the fabric and board.
***This right angle is important.*** .......... as it correctly aligns the seams. When all pins are firmly stuck in, push the fabric down onto the board's surface.

3.  Lift the top fabric layer and place a piece of double sided sticky tape over each crossing seam. Replace the top layer of fabric and press it firmly  onto the tape. This simple action will hold the seams in the correct position  allowing you to safely  flip the pins ready for stitching

4.  Stitch the seam in the usual way. Remove both pins and  tape. ( I usually stick each piece to the table edge for use  at least once more.)

**The order of sewing is as follows......**

a. Small sections which make up the patterns within a tile should be sewn first.
b. Tiles should be sewn together to form wedge shaped strips.
c. Strips should be sewn together to form  floor, ceiling or wall sections.
d. Sections should be sewn together to complete the patchwork.
e. The landscape is completed separately.
f. Landscape and patchwork are joined together.
g. Borders are added if required.

## *Assembling The Patchwork Surround.*

Ceiling, floor and wall sections of the surround should be completed separately ready for joining.

***When joining floor, ceiling and wall sections leave the last outer 1/2 in. of the seams open  if a mitred border is to be attached.*** ......... (see p 75.)

When all the seams are sewn, the paper design will be complete again on the back .... just like a jig-saw puzzle....

(in theory the paper can be used again, if you can figure out a storage method which will prevent  getting the pieces muddled ....
otherwise it could lead to insanity ...  fast !!)

When the perspective patchwork is complete put it aside until the landscape is finished.

> **Do not remove the freezer paper at this stage.**

## Stitching the Scene.

The most important fact to remember before you embark upon the task of stitching the landscape is that the scene will be reversed by the stitching process. Check that your particular scene has been drafted correctly ........

**i.e.  Real places must be reversed  by  the design process ... see p 32.**
**Imaginary scenes ... it doesn't matter ...... as no one will know.**

There are three assembly options to choose from. These affect the number of seams sewn  and therefore the length of time needed to complete the item.

1. The simplest and fastest option is to cut each section from one fabric. The vanishing lines can then be quilted, embroidered or sprayed to achieve the perspective effect.

2. Another choice might be to piece some sections and not others.

3.  Lastly you may decide to piece all sections to maximise the linear and aerial perspective effect, by the patchwork of fabric used.

---

**Tip.**

It is a good idea to  draw a quick 'thumbnail  sketch' of the landscape, numbering the various sections, just in case you get confused during the construction process.  Cut one section away from the scene at a time to complete, before going on to the next. I pin all  finished sections  in position  on  a design  wall so that I can clearly see the developing picture.

---

The techniques used to complete the scene vary from those used for the perspective patchwork. This is because more irregular shapes will be joined, many with curved edges. However, no conventional curved seams need to be sewn. Everything will be stitched from the right side providing  perfect visibility at all times  and eliminating any guesswork.

Once again the freezer paper will act as a stabiliser throughout the assembly process. At times the stitching will be sewn through the paper as well as the fabric, following the  vanishing lines which provide an exact guide to accuracy.
If you choose, fabric can be pieced  e.g. stripped colours,  before the freezer paper is ironed to the wrong side, thus increasing the complexity of design achieved.

---

*Remember* ............. the colour sequence is the same as before ....
strong colours at the front (the top and bottom of the scene)
graduating to the palest colours on the horizon.

**Sew and Flip.**

This is an easy way to piece individual section of landscape, ensuring that the seam lines fall very accurately on the vanishing lines. The lines drawn on the paper sections are the guidelines for the stitching.

1.  Take the chosen  landscape section, and the appropriate fabric colour selection it will contain. Each wedge shaped section between vanishing lines could contain a different   fabric ........ or a few can be chosen and repeated as necessary. To save many thread colour changes, choose a mid grey .. this will blend with everything.

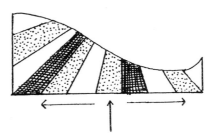

2.  The application of fabric will begin in the wedge space which  falls roughly in the middle of the paper section.  Thereafter fabric will be added on  both sides of this first piece.

---

**Tip.**

The most efficient way to cut the fabric prior to application is in strips ......
double checking that the cut width is sufficient to fill the wedge space
*plus a minimum 1/2 in.*  for the seam allowances on both sides.
*The pieces do not have to be cut to shape*  ...
They will be sewn to the correct shape as the stitching progresses.

---

3.  The right side of the design will be viewed from the shiny side of the freezer paper throughout the assembly process ......  all fabric pieces will be added from that side.
The sewing lines will be visible on the dull side. The dull side should  therefore be *uppermost*   every time a seam is sewn.

4.  Iron the first fabric piece behind the appropriate wedge space on the freezer paper ... shiny side of the paper against the wrong side of the fabric as usual.

Check that it completely covers the space and has sufficient seam allowance on either side.


*The fabric must  also exceed  the paper at the top and bottom by at least 1/4 in.*

5.  Stitch through the paper following the vanishing lines on either side of the wedge.
*Do not stitch exactly on top of the  drawn lines ...  but fractionally outside the wedge.* ....... i.e. marginally to the right of the line  on the right .........
and marginally to the left of the line on the left.

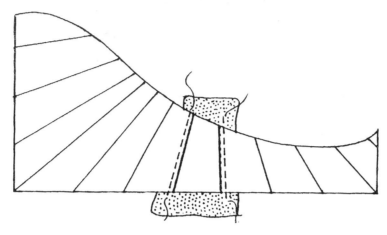

The purpose of this stitching  (which will be repeated each time a new piece of fabric is added)  is ....

a. To anchor the fabric while the seam allowances on either side  are trimmed to shape.

b. To reinforce the seam stitching so that it will not distort or weaken when the freezer paper is removed.

6.  Fold the paper back on itself  on top of one of the stitching lines, and unstick the seam allowance fabric beyond. Using the fold as a guide, trim the allowance to 1/4 in.  Repeat on the other side. Straighten out the paper section.

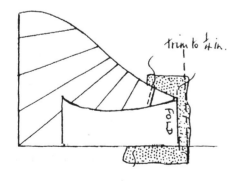

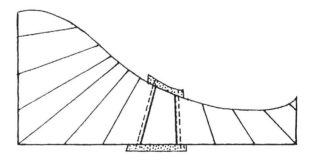

All fabric pieces added after the first are added right sides together with the previous one. This means that the wrong side will temporarily face out.
(When it has been stitched in place it will be folded back into its  correct position with the right side facing out.)

7.  Take the next piece of fabric, position it so that the edge corresponds with that of one of the previously trimmed seam allowances. Use pins to hold it in place. Double check that when it is folded back, after stitching, it will definitely be big enough to cover ......   a.  the entire neighbouring wedge, *plus*

                        b.  the side seam allowance,   *and*

                        c.  the 1/4 in top and bottom.

(This is an estimate that everyone gets wrong at the beginning if they're not careful. It always seems to be wider than you think .... so be generous !)

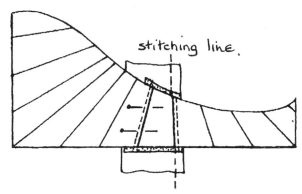

stitching line.

8.  Stitch through the paper exactly on top of the vanishing line you stitched alongside last time. This new stitching will accurately outline one side of the wedge. The previous stitching will be invisible when the fabric is flipped back.

9. Flip the new fabric piece into position covering the next wedge, pin it in place.

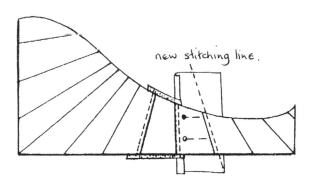

new stitching line.

10. Sew through the paper to anchor this new fabric in position by stitching marginally outside the next vanishing line. Fold the paper and trim the seam allowance as before. Remove the pins and select the next piece of fabric.

11.  Repeat to cover every wedge on the paper section working to the right and left of the first. Make sure that the wedges at the edges of the paper overlap by at least 1/4 in. all around.

12.  Complete all the pieced sections in the landscape in this way. Press them flat. If the section is made up of only one fabric ... complete it by ironing the freezer paper template to the fabric, (shiny side to the wrong side) and cut with 1/4 in. seam allowance all around.

# Completing the Landscape.

When all the individual landscape elements are sewn or ironed to the freezer paper, either as plain fabric or pieced sections, they are ready to be joined together.

The freezer paper templates have been cut to actual size and the seam allowances are extra all around. Therefore all the freezer paper edges will match together as they did for the patchwork section, however this time all the sewing will be completed from the right side, making all those curves a "piece of cake." Each time curves are to be joined, one seam allowance will be folded over the paper, while the other will remain flat. The folded one will be sewn from the right side, on top of the flat one, using a fine machine needle, straight stitching and invisible thread ............ an easy route to a great finish.

**Method.**

1. Take two neighbouring landscape sections. It is always easier to fold the seam allowance over on the one with the hill tops along the edge to be joined. As these are convex curves, the seam allowance will not need to be clipped as it would around concave edges. If there is a mixture of both, clip the concave curves and points at 1/4 in. intervals ........ almost, ... but not quite up to the paper. These cuts must be invisible when the allowance is folded.

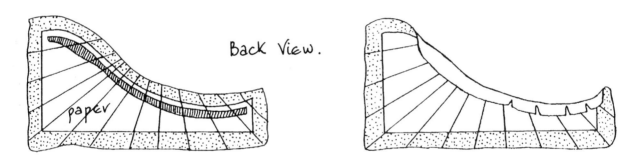

Back View.

2.   The easy way to anchor the folded fabric to the paper is to use a little Spray Mount adhesive. This is an aerosol, non staining, tacky glue available from art suppliers.  (It will last a long time, as very little is required.)

Spray a small amount into a saucer and then apply to the paper in a line following the  curves. Do this either with a finger or a small brush. Keep the glue away from the extreme edge of the paper. This is where the machine needle will pierce during the stitching. Fold the fabric over the paper's  edge, with the tip of a warm iron, pressing it firmly in place. It will be held down for as long as necessary, and the fabric can easily be unstuck after stitching to remove the paper.

3.   Lay the folded edge in place on top of it's neighbour's  seam allowance. The exact positioning, (matching paper's edge to paper's edge) can be checked by holding the sections up to the light, or by pushing a pin through both, to check the alignment. Pin the sections together when correctly positioned.

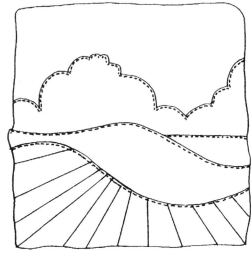

4. Straight stitch the sections together, following the curves, as near as possible to the folded edge. If the machine is set to sew a short stitch length, and a fine needle and transparent thread are used, the stitching will be almost invisible.

(Use a size 60 needle for completing an 'heirloom,' .... for everything else size 70, as they are less inclined to break.)

5. Sections which have a straight seam between them .......... e.g. the top of a water section, can also be joined in the same way.

6. Join all the sections in this way to complete the landscape

7. The base of trees, bushes, clouds and other additional features, can be inserted into the seams between individual pieced sections of landscape and sky. Appliqué stitching around the remainder of the shape need not be completed at this time, it can be finished off when the background is complete.

**Freezer Paper Appliqué Technique ....... for adding trees, bushes. clouds etc.**

a. The paper shape is cut to the exact size. Iron it shiny side down to the wrong side of the fabric.

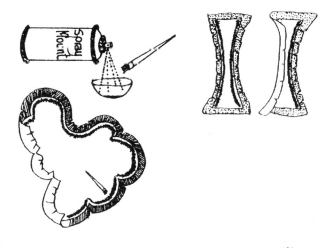

b. The seam allowance is added when the fabric is cut.

c. Put 'Spray Mount' in a line around the edge of the shape with a brush or finger.

d. Fold the fabric edge over the paper and press to the 'Spray Mount' with the tip of a warm iron. Clip concave edges.

e. Stitch in place around the edge using a blind hemstitch, small zig- zag or straight stitching.

f. On completion, turn the landscape to the wrong side and cut away the background fabric to 1/4 in of the stitching and remove the paper.

**Appliqué clouds and Vegetation......**

Fine detail is difficult in the technique of appliqué. If it is required it is best added by using ........

a.    appropriately printed fabric.... (see 'Deeper Still' on page 38,) where the landscape contains printed trees and hills ..... or....
b.  machine or hand embroidery ....... ( See 'Terra Australis' on page 49.)

Fabric shapes for appliqué are approximate, suggesting an overall shape rather than accurately reproducing exact appearance.

Curves of mixed size are easy to use for clouds. hedges and trees.

Look closely at tree shapes when you are out and about.

A landscape without patchwork surround is now complete. Remove the freezer paper, and add borders or not, as you wish prior to quilting.

*Landscapes with a surround ... Do not remove the freezer paper yet !!*

# *Joining The Patchwork To The Landscape.*

With both patchwork and landscape sections now complete, the next step is to join them together. If conventional methods were to be used it could be difficult to match all the vanishing line seams. Luckily there is an easier way ..... by fusing the edges together prior to stitching.

On inspecting the back of each completed section the 1/4 in. seam allowance can be seen beyond the paper, all around the outside edges. The same will be noticed along the patchwork edge which will be joined to the landscape. Therefore, at present there is 1/2 in. overlap between the sections at this edge, equal to the combination of both these allowances. This double overlap provides extra 'insurance' should one allowance be a little short.
(The benefit of having the paper stuck to the fabric at this stage is that the width of the seam allowances can be double checked.)

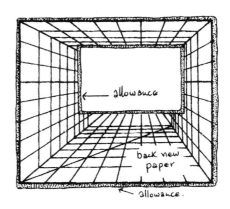

**Method.**

1. Cut the 1/4 in. allowance from the edge of the *landscape* which is to be joined to the patchwork.

### Yes ..... cut the seam allowance off !!!

**But before you start cutting remember.....**

- only cut at the edges where landscape is to be joined to patchwork.

- a full 1/4 in. overlap between landscape and patchwork is required.

- it is a good idea to check in position ... trim a little and check again.

- In designs where the patchwork completely surrounds the landscape the whole outer edge will be trimmed.

- If the edge is straight, use a rotary cutter and ruler to make sure that the cut is perfectly straight and the corners are right angles.

**When trimming is complete the freezer paper can be removed** from both the landscape and patchwork sections.

Do this with care, so that the cut edges will not be frayed as you go.
If the paper has been accidentally stitched through, tear it along beside the stitching line where it has been perforated ........... take care not to distort the stitching.

A little fusible webbing is now required.
"Bondaweb" ... or "Wonder Under" gives me the best results.

2. Cut enough "Bondaweb" into 1/4 in. strips to go around the perimeter of the landscape.

3. Iron the strips to the landscape edge, placing the webbing against the wrong side of the fabric. Place the pressing sheet beneath the fabric to prevent any webbing which may overlap from sticking to your ironing board.

4.  Position the landscape on top of the patchwork. Match and pin seam lines where appropriate.

5.  Carefully fuse the landscape on top of the patchwork using a moderately hot iron. This will make a temporary but secure join, whilst awaiting the stitching.

6.  Stitch around the edge of the landscape using a very small zig zag stitch. (Approximately machine setting 2 on both stitch length and width.) This will make the join permanent and prevent fraying. I usually complete this stage using transparent thread on the top so that it is almost invisible and has very little bulk.

7.  If you have included some ' escaping vegetation' in your design it can now be pinned and appliqué stitched in place overlapping this zig-zagged join.

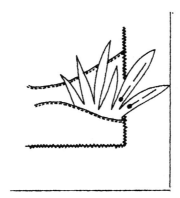

8. This join can now be finished off with a line of decorative satin stitch which completely covers the previous zig-zag. The stitch width is up to the designer as is the choice of a toning or contrasting colour thread.

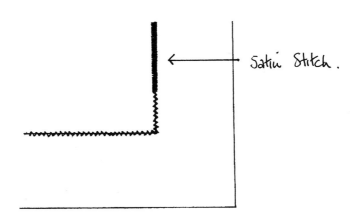

Satin Stitch.

**'Connemara Lily.'** by Angela Madden.

70

**'Captain Cook and I.'**     38 x 50 ins.     by Angela Madden.

This quilt uses lovely hand dyed New Zealand fabric in the water, and the national fern symbol is quilted in the border.

# *Designing A Border.*

The combined landscape and patchwork can be completed with either a binding or a border around the edge. One or more borders will frame and enlarge the design, providing scope for additional patchwork or quilting ideas.

However, borders need a little more thought in these designs, than they do on more conventional quilts.........

The perspective effect in many designs results in corner angles which are split unevenly by the major corner vanishing lines .... i.e. in 90° corners the vanishing lines do not create a 45° mitre. In fact all four corner angles in any one design are usually split differently, (unless the focal point of a design has been placed exactly in the middle.)

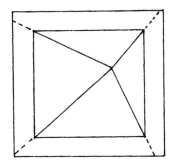

If a uniform width border were to be sewn around a typical perspective design it would not be possible to continue the corner lines of the design into the border, and have the corner seams ending at the points.

At first glance this might look like a problem. Again there is an easy solution ...........
and several alternative options to choose from .......

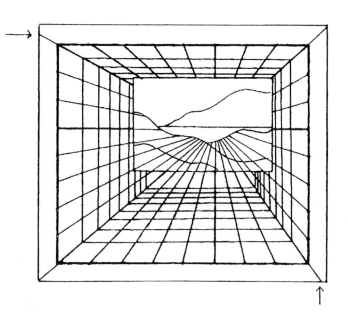

a.   A uniform width border with irregular corners. ..............
This can look interesting and make people  wonder how you worked it out !

b. A uniform width border with a decorative square placed at each corner. The border can be any width you choose.

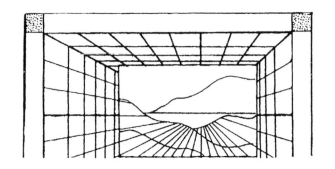

c. A uniform width tiled border. This time the width must equal the calibrations around the outside edge (plus seam allowances.) The tiles would be the same divisions around the outside edge of the design. The tiles could be used in different ways to create...........

1. *A two colour chequer board effect* .........
(There will always be an even number of border tiles ....
around a complete border.)
**Note ..** that if a two colour chequer board effect has been used throughout the patchwork, this border will not work out correctly at the corners.

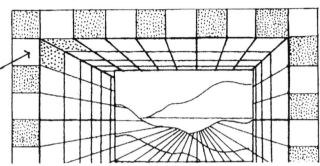

2. **A *multi coloured tiled effect*** ...........

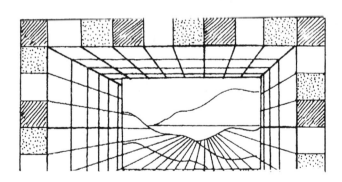

3. *A continuation of the block pattern* used in the perspective patchwork.

All these alternatives create the effect of stopping the perspective and returning the design to a flat plane. It now appears as if a wall or frame surrounds the view. All these options could also be completed as border quilting designs, using coloured threads to echo the pieced design .....
see 'Connemara lily 'quilt on page 70 .

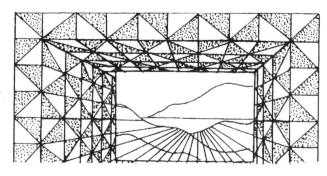

d.  Varied width borders ....... this alternative enables the landscape corner seams to continue from the design ending exactly in the corners of the border. This looks mathematical and complicated .... again there's an easy way around it !

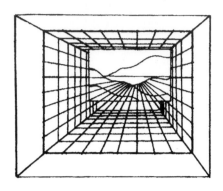

## *Attaching the borders.*

1.   Borders which have a square tile at the corners are attached by adding strips to the top and bottom of the quilt omitting the corner tiles. The two side strips are then added with a corner tile stitched to both ends, completing the border.

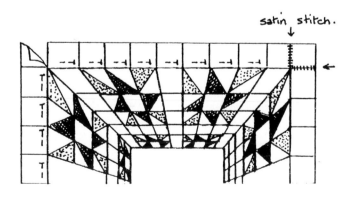

2.  Tiled border strips must be matched at each tile seam. Once again, the easiest method of attaching the strips is to secure them with fusible webbing prior to satin stitching. This facilitates stress free seam matching, as it can all be done with full visibility from the top.
A 1/4 in. strip of fusible should be ironed to the trimmed edge of all border strips. This will overlap the outer 1/4 in. seam allowance of the patchwork pattern.

3. Tiled border strips can be pinned and matched at each tile seam, ready for fusing with a moderately hot dry iron.

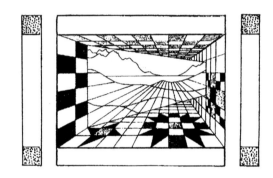

satin stitch.

4. The corner squares will end up with one seam fused and one stitched. This will not matter as the satin stitching which will finish off the fused edge can be repeated over the stitched seam and both will then look the same.

5. Borders which have mitred corners, (whether they are at 45°on not,) are added as four separate, equal width strips in any order. It is essential that the strip length equals the quilt side measurement ....... plus twice the strip width and a little extra.

6. Mitred seams will now benefit from the unsewn 1/2 in. left at each corner when the patchwork sections were assembled, (p 59.)  so that they can be separated at the corners. The fusible is ironed to the edge of each strip as above. Border strips are attached along the full length of all quilt sides.

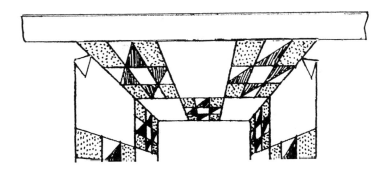

7. Taking one corner at a time, fold one border strip out of the way exposing its neighbour. Position a rotary cutting ruler across this border in line with the corner angle of the patchwork. The seam should lie exactly 1/4 in. from the ruler's edge, allowing you to cut the border 1/4 in. in excess of whatever angle the seam happens to create. The excess will be the allowance, when angled seam is sewn to complete the corner. Cut all border strips in this way.

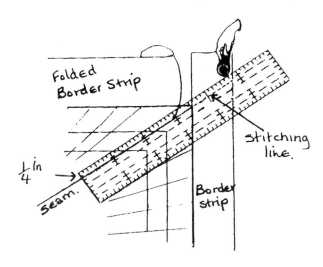

8. Fold each corner of the quilt top in turn along the seam, aligning the cut ends of the border strips. Sew a continuation of the patchwork corner seam across the border to complete both patchwork and border corners.

This method of cutting the mitre will work whatever the angle in the patchwork.

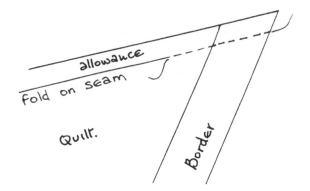

9. With these seams completed on equal width borders it will be apparent that the seams may not finish exactly in the corners. The individual seam angles will determine this ...... only a 45° angle reaches the corner tip. If you are happy with this effect ... that's fine.

If not ... it can easily be altered by changing the width of individual borders at this stage. Trim each border in turn so that the seam finishes in the exact corner. Frequently all four borders will then be of different widths, which will further enhance the perspective illusion. The small amount of fabric wastage incurred by this trimming is outweighed by the speed and ease of this method. (See the borders in 'Connemara lily' p 70. )

## Quilting Ideas.

There are several methods of quilting which will further enhance the perspective effect of these quilts.
Consider the following .......

1. Quilting 'in the ditch' along the vanishing lines from the patchwork into the landscape maximises the perspective effect. Such quilted lines can cross unpieced sections of land, sea or sky, echoing the piecing and moving the viewer's eye towards the focal point. Spaces between vanishing lines can be textured using quilted filler patterns.

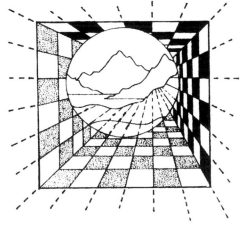

2. Plain tiles can be given a textured patchwork appearance by quilting block patterns onto them. This effect can be further increased by using coloured thread. The free machining 'Vermicelli ' pattern ( Sew with the machine 'feed-dog' in the down position) is ideal for this and well worth a bit of practice to gain confidence and control.

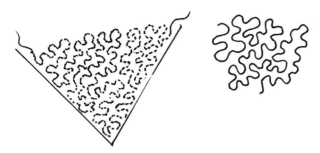 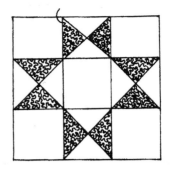

3. Borders can also be used as areas in which block designs can be quilted. These can continue the pieced design from the patchwork section, once again maximising the perspective effect.

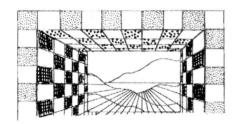 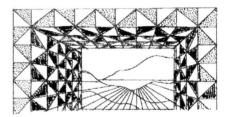

4. I like to use appropriate motifs, which are quilted in contrasting coloured thread as part of the border design.
These occur in 'Pink ice' on page 50. (Snowflakes) .....
'Captain Cook and I,' on page 71. (New Zealand Ferns) ......    and ......
'Into the Dawn' on page  52. (Stars)

The motif outlines are  drawn on the fabric around a cardboard template, using a sharp coloured pencil, or chalk. This provides a clear line to follow with the machine straight stitch. The inner detail can then be completed by free machining. Both the stars and ferns were sewn in this way.

The snowflakes were first drawn onto thin tracing (or greaseproof) paper, pinned in place and free stitched, following the pattern lines, sewing through both paper and quilt. The paper was then torn away. This method eliminates the need to mark the design on the fabric.

Areas around the motifs can be filled in with textural quilting patterns in either transparent thread, or one matched to the fabric colour.

5. Another idea that appeals to me is that of changing the colour of fabric in a subtle way by using closely quilted designs in contrasting thread. This is especially effective in plain graduation dyed  fabric. See the border of  'Connemara Lilies' on page  70.  Also see the border of  'Captain Cook and I' ... page 71, where the thread colour in both the ferns and background quilting varies, responding to changes in the colour of the fabric behind .... light thread on dark fabric and vise versa.

## A Few Dimensional Ideas.

We have looked so far at ways of creating a 3 D. illusion on a flat surface, in these quilt designs. It therefore seems appropriate  to mention the possible inclusion of raised elements which add real dimensional interest.
These could be ........... embroidery, either by machine or hand .....
manipulated fabric, ruched or folded, .......
or 3D. appliqué.  ....... A close look at the pictured examples will show all of these.

You might like to try .......

1.  Crochet cotton (hand wound,) in the machine bobbin. If the cotton bypasses the bobbin tension spring, this can be sewn using a standard thread in the needle.

In machines which have a bobbin case, the cotton is fed straight through the larger hole in the case and not  brought through the  side slit.

In machines which have  top loading bobbins, the thread is brought up from the bobbin without threading it round the side channel.

The thick thread will sew on the lower side of the work so the quilt is placed in the machine with the top side underneath.You will need clear guidance from existing quilting lines so that you are certain to be stitching in the right place. The cow parsley in the quilt 'Butterfly Spring' on the inside front cover, was done in this way, providing both colour and textural contrast to the surrounding fabric.

2.  Raw edged Appliqué ... as in  the vegetation 'Aspect on Delft' page  34. and pine trees in 'Alpine holiday' page 35.  In both these examples single fabric has been attached with a minimum of stitching so that the raw edge hangs loose, and the slightly frayed edge adds texture.

3.  3D. turned flowers and butterflies ... see 'Arran' on page 36, and ' Butterfly Spring' on the inside front cover.  Double fabric shapes have been edge stitched, right sides together, then turned through a central cut slit, before appliquéing to the design. The inclusion of a little stuffing will further add to the effect.

# The Finishing Touch.

When your quilt is finally completed it is time to stand back to admire your handiwork. However, it sometimes seems that no matter how carefully the quilt top was ironed, or how much effort has gone into the project, it looks a bit 'lumpy' and refuses to lie flat, or or hang as straight as you would wish.
'Blocking' the project could solve this last problem.

**Method.**

1.  Lie the quilt down on a carpeted floor.

2.  Push pins through the quilt, straight down into the carpet all along one edge, positioning them in a line just inside the binding.

3.  Repeat on the opposite edge, giving the quilt a pull as you go,  placing it under tension. Check that the correct shape is being maintained .... sometimes  a 'dent' in the side, or a short corner might need a stronger pull to correct it. Uneven amounts of quilting can often cause parts of a quilt to buckle, leaving some edges shorter than others. Blocking will not cure wild discrepancies .... but it can always improve.

4.  Pin the remaining two sides in the same way. It is a good idea to check the measurements as you go, to ensure that, if there is a problem, you are not pulling it further out of shape.

5.  Dampen the quilt with a water spray ........ ( ideally all fabrics will have been washed, however, if this is not the case, spray lightly, watching very carefully for any sign of colour bleeding,)  I have never had a problem with shrinkage, as all, fabrics are held under tension until the quilt is completely dry, ideally overnight.

6.  Blocking is also good for removing any wrinkles, or fold lines which may result from storage.

7.  Finally when the fabric is completely dry give it another light spray with starch .... allowing it to dry again before removing the pins. This encourages the quilt to retain its flat, unwrinkled appearance. I hold the spray can with the hole in the nozzle pointing upwards so that the starch is not sprayed  densely on the fabric.

*Blocking a quilt can considerably improve its appearance, making a good quilt look great ... and a problem quilt more acceptable.*

I sincerely hope that you will create many great quilts with these techniques, and enjoy many happy hours sewing along the way.

## By the same Author.

*'Sew Easy Celtic'......* The easiest ever way to learn to design your own Celtic knotwork patterns for needlework and other crafts. Absolutely no artistic or mathematical skill needed for brilliant, fast, machine sewn results. Based on drawing symmetrical doodles .... so everyone can do it using this book!

*'Magic Celtic'...* More easy designing ... this book uses more doodles, to create original, multi-sectional knotwork designs .... they look amazingly complicated... but are easy to draft, and fast to machine sew.

*'Appliqué and Roses'.....* An appliqué technique for block and border design. This book shows how to easily create limitless original patterns. Fast machine sewing.
The same principles can be applied to drafting vine designs also ..... with a new, multiple production system for adding 3D roses and leaves. Forget copying other peoples patterns ... be original ..... create your own in half the time!

*'Slice up a Circle'.......* The easy book of 'geometricks' for patchworkers ( especially non- mathematicians). Endless original designs can be created, then painlessly assembled with very accurate results. If you've ever admired a brilliant geometric designed quilt at a show and wondered how it was done ... this book is for you.

*The 'Circle Slice Ruler'.....* for use with 'Slice up a Circle' and also 'Magic Celtic' ..... takes all the inaccuracy out of drafting precise angles for multi - sectional designing. Throw away your protractor ... this is much easier to use.

*The ' Multi - Plait' Tool.....* another new tool which helps you to draft plaits ( braids ) quickly and accurately in different styles and sizes. These patterns are suitable for quilting, embroidery, applique or bias appliqué, for both block and border designs using varying numbers of cords. It too, is really easy and speedy to use ... and it even takes plaits correctly around corners for you!

*The 'Designer Feather Tool'....* Traditional feathered wreathes, borders, hearts, squares etc. are universally popular designs. This tool is the essential aid to fast, original drafting ......... feather any shape and in any size for quilting, embroidery, appliqué and bias appliqué.

*If sewing isn't easy, successful and fun ... why do it?*

**If you have difficulty in obtaining any of the above please contact either the publisher ... or ... the international distributors listed in the front of this book..**